S0-BCN-645

NORTHERN GNOSIS

For Pete
With thanks!
best
Cy Mogensen

SPRING JOURNAL BOOKS
STUDIES IN ARCHETYPAL PSYCHOLOGY SERIES

Series Editor
GREG MOGENSON

OTHER TITLES IN THE SERIES

DIALECTICS & ANALYTICAL PSYCHOLOGY:
THE EL CAPITAN CANYON SEMINAR
Wolfgang Giegerich, David L. Miller, Greg Mogenson

RAIDS ON THE UNTHINKABLE:
FREUDIAN & JUNGIAN PSYCHOANALYSES
Paul Kugler

THE NEUROSIS OF PSYCHOLOGY:
PRIMARY PAPERS TOWARDS A CRITICAL PSYCHOLOGY
(FORTHCOMING, OCTOBER 2005)
Wolfgang Giegerich

NORTHERN GNOSIS

*Thor, Baldr, and the Volsungs
in the Thought of Freud
and Jung*

Greg Mogenson

Spring Journal Books
New Orleans, Louisiana

© 2005 by Greg Mogenson.
All rights reserved.

Published by
Spring Journal, Inc.;
627 Ursulines Street #7
New Orleans, Louisiana 70116
Tel.: (504) 524-5117
Fax: (504) 558-0088
Website: www.springjournalandbooks.com

Printed in Canada.
Text printed on acidfree paper.

Cover image
adapted from a woodcut
(see facing page)
by
Hans Gerhard Sørensen

Cover design by
Northern Cartographic
4050 Williston Road
South Burlington, Vermont 05403

Library in Congress Cataloging in Publication Data
Pending

Woodcut by Hans Gerhard Sørensen

For

Michael Mendis

Contents

Acknowledgments

I want to thank my colleagues Ron Schenk, John Desteian, and Anita Chapman for their stimulating and generative support while I was writing this book. Nancy Cater, the publisher of Spring Journal Books, has been a wonderful collaborator on this and other projects, for which I thank her warmly. Thanks are also due to Michael Mendis for his help with the manuscript production, Ragnhild Talman for assistance with the illustrations, and to my wife, Rita Mendis-Mogenson, for her love and support.

Chapter two of this book, in a slightly different version, was previously published as a two-part article, "Barnstock's Progeny: The Sword of Incest and the Tree of Life in Freud, Jung, and Spielrein," which appeared in *Quadrant: Journal of the C. G. Jung Foundation for Analytical Psychology* (Vol. XX, no. 2, 2000, pp. 20-41 & Vol. XXI, no. 1, 2001, pp. 31-47). The author and publisher gratefully acknowledge permission to reprint this article.

The woodcut print illustration, "Odin's Sacrifice," on p. xvii is by Pete White of Murrieta, California.

All other illustrations are woodcuts by Hans Gerhard Sørensen.

The author and publisher gratefully acknowledge the permission of Pete White and Brit Anne Sørensen to reprint these works.

Introduction

One word led me
to other words.
One work led me
to other works.[1]

—Óðinn

The story is told that Óðinn gouged out one of his own eyes as
a sacrifice for the gift of wisdom. Haemorrhaging visions, the
gory orb gazed out from Mirmir's well, the spring that feeds
the World Tree, Yggdrasill, which houses the nine worlds. To sacrifice
an eye in the manner of this Northern All-Father of the Gods is to
dedicate the mind to a particular way of comprehending things. It is
to take up an idea in a committed way and to see it through. The
Óðinn's eye of an idea that we shall be taking up in these pages comes
from Jung. Reflecting upon psychology in the light of his concept of
the archetype (an idea for which he, too, had given an eye), the great
psychologist writes,

> Psychology, as one of the many expressions of psychic life,
> operates with ideas which in their turn are derived from
> archetypal structures and thus generate a somewhat more
> abstract kind of myth. Psychology therefore translates the
> archaic speech of myth into a modern mythologem—not
> yet, of course, recognized as such—which constitutes one
> element of the myth "science." This seemingly hopeless
> undertaking is a *living and lived myth*, satisfying to persons
> of a corresponding temperament, indeed, beneficial in so far
> as they have been cut off from their psychic origins by
> neurotic dissociation.[2]

---

[1] From the *Hávamál* of the *Elder Edda*, stanza 140.
[2] C. G. Jung, *Collected Works*, tr. R. F. C. Hull (Princeton, NJ: Princeton University
Press, 1953), vol. 9, i, para. 302 (all subsequent references to Jung's *Collected Works*,
vols. 1-20, will be by volume—*CW*—and paragraph number—§).

Our endeavour in the chapters that follow will be to demonstrate that the archaic speech of myth has, indeed, been translated into a modern mythologem—that "living and lived myth," as Jung calls it, psychology. A comparative study, our approach shall be one of insighting the theories of Freud and Jung through the lens of Norse myth. In keeping with this focus, our interest will be less in providing a psychological reading of Norse mythology than in discovering how the Norse divinities enact themselves in the concepts and theories of our depth psychological forebears.

The myths of our Northern ancestors were a vital expression of their struggle to exist in the world in which they found themselves. Psychology, like the cycle of ancient stories which preceded it, is equally this for us. It, too, is a myth, even as the myths of the ancient North were the psychology of a past era.[3] Of course, there are differences. History has moved on; times have changed. We are divided from the meaning that myth had in the past by an enormous gulf. And, yet, the comparisons that can be drawn have a vitalizing effect upon the practice of psychology and analysis. Simply by calling psychology a myth (and recognizing in this way its symbolic dimension) we establish a living connection to its theories, using them in a different way than we would if we valued them only for their explanatory power. *Cum grano salis*, it is now up to psychology to be for our time what *I-Ching* hexagrams, Norse runes, and just-so stories were for another.

From its earliest beginnings, the tradition of depth psychology has been fascinated with mythology. This fascination, however, has for the most part taken the form of *interpreting* the myths. Listening to the ancient stories as if they had been spoken from the mouth of a patient, psychology treated them to its talking cure. Mostly, this consisted of simple translation work. Myth's images and motifs were explained in terms of whatever theoretical terms were current in psychology. Ironically, however, these terms were often much more than simply concepts with which to think. Reified and hallowed, they functioned, for all their abstractness, as gods themselves.

A connection may here be drawn to how in mythology an older order of divinities is frequently supplanted by a subsequent one—the Vanir by the Æsir in Norse mythology, the Titans by the Olympians in Greek

---

[3] Cf. James Hillman, *The Dream and the Underworld* (New York: Harper & Row, 1979), p. 22. See also James Hillman, *Re-Visioning Psychology* (New York: Harper & Row, 1975), p. 20.

mythology. Heir to the myths that preceded it, psychology has yet to work through its own version of this archetypal pattern. I refer, of course, to the battle of the god-terms in the annals of psychoanalysis. Beginning with the parting of the ways between Freud and Jung, and continued between the various schools of analysis, this battle may have its root in the failure of depth psychology to recognize that the theories of its founders are just so many new heads sprung from the age-old hydra of myth. With the hindsight of a century, however, it now seems an irony that Freud, while loathing the "black tide of mud ... of occultism"[4] which he feared Jung's research into mythology might release, found all our beginnings in Oedipus and created a pantheon of concepts with names such as Ego and Id, Eros and Thanatos (as his followers later called his death-instinct) even as his estranged colleague went on to conceive of the psyche as a series of encounters with such *dramatis personae* as the shadow and the anima. While both men made their respective contributions to the new mythologem of psychology by means of a shift from the imaginal language of the ancient myths to more or less abstract conceptualizations of that language, each was at the same time inspired by what he sensed the other had left out in the process.[5] That each theorist continued in his own way to allow the imaginal to inform his thinking bears witness to the fecundity of the unknowable object which they both designated with the god-terms "psyche" and "the unconscious."

At the forefront of the image-oriented thought which has followed in the wake of Jung's characterization of psychology as a modern mythologem is the work of James Hillman. Inspired by Jung's idea that both psychology and mythology are underpinned by common archetypes, Hillman's "post-Jungian" school of archetypal psychology has attempted nothing less that a full-scale "re-visioning of psychology" from the perspective of Greek polytheism.[6] By returning to the stories of the various divinities of the classical period for background to its imaginings, archetypal psychology has sought to reconnect the notion of the archetype with the concrete images and specific details of the myths themselves. The innovation here is the notion that images have depth

---

[4] C. G. Jung, *Memories, Dreams, Reflections*, ed. A. Jaffé (New York: Random House), p. 150.

[5] Cf. Freud's charge that Jung had "failed to hear the mighty and primordial melody of the instincts." *The Standard Edition of the Complete Psychological Works of Sigmund Freud*, tr. J. Strachey, vol. XIV (London: Hogarth Press, 1961), p. 62.

[6] James Hillman, *Re-Visioning Psychology*.

and meaning in and of themselves.[7] Jung, approaching images through his technique of amplification, moved away from the specificity of particular images. For him, the likeness between various mythic images pointed to the existence of otherwise irrepresentable archetypes.[8] It was largely by elucidating these structures that Jung translated the archaic speech of myth into the conceptual language of analytical psychology. In contrast to this approach, archetypal psychology's return to myth has been a return to the image. By adhering more strictly to Jung's dictum— "image *is* psyche"[9]—than Jung himself tended to, archetypal psychology has shown that images need not be related to more abstractly conceived symbols to be meaningful.[10]

My own approach in these pages owes much to Hillman and to archetypal psychology. Mimetic to the work of this school, I, too, shall be turning to myths for perspective and re-visioning psychology from the perspective of specific mythic images. A difference, however, is that my return to myth is simultaneously a return to the concepts and theories of Freud and Jung. My interest, in contrast to Hillman's, is in the re-discovery of the writings of these theorists as myths, and of their concepts as images.[11] In a sense, my intent is to play both ends of the so-called classical-archetypal continuum of analytical psychology against the middle. While on the one hand, in line with Hillman's approach, I attempt to stay with specific images and imagine in terms of the perspectives that they offer, on the other hand I retain something of the conceptual vocabulary of Freud and Jung, terms such as "objective psyche," "the unconscious," and "psychic reality." While Hillman has moved away from these terms, preferring to speak of image and imagination instead, my own proclivity is to retain them. From my perspective, concepts are as valuable as images, even *are* images. They, too, resound with archetypal depth. Just as one image implies another, thereby activating the living fantasies that animate our psychic life, so concepts can open into one another.

---

[7] James Hillman, *Archetypal Psychology: A Brief Account* (Dallas: Spring Publications, 1983), pp. 11-15.

[8] Jung, *CW* 11 § 222.

[9] Jung, *CW* 13 § 75.

[10] Hillman, *Archetypal Psychology*, pp. 6-15.

[11] Hillman laid the ground work for this approach in a work in which he compares Freud's account of the unconscious with the underworld of Greek mythology. See his *The Dream and the Underworld* (New York: Harper & Row, 1979), pp. 7-22.

There is another important contrast between my approach and that of Hillman, and this concerns what Hillman calls "cultural locus."[12] Archetypal psychology, according to Hillman, "starts in the South," which is to say, in the same imaginal Mediterranean soil from which Greek and Renaissance civilization sprang.[13] In this study, by contrast, we shall return to the North. This shift of cultural locus, like Hillman's contrary one, is consistent with the intent of our venture. Just as archetypal psychology, hoping to free itself from the conceptual terms in which depth psychology has come to be literalized, turned to the South in order to situate itself in a "pre-psychological geography" in which what the North formulated as "psychology" was implicit to the culture of imagination and very mode of life,[14] we, hoping to return to the concepts and theories of Freud and Jung as to the living and lived myth of our time, return to the landscapes of Northern Europe. The North we return to, however, is not only that of twentieth-century Zürich and Vienna—the North which Hillman left behind. Our North is also the ancient, pagan North of Thor, Baldr, and the Volsungs.

Psychology, according to Jung, is necessarily a subjective confession of its author, a product or function of his inner experience. This is true, not only for the author, but for the reader as well. The resonance between the myths of the North and the writings of Freud and Jung is first and foremost a felt experience. Just as the wonders of the natural world evoke reactions in us which are commensurate with their grandeur, so one may experience the numinosum in one's armchair with one's books. Affects get constellated, and one underlines a sentence. Or, seeing a connection with another text, one excitedly scribbles a note in the margin. As if by a bolt from the blue, one has been struck by what Jung, in a particularly apt definition of what he meant by the term "numinous," called "*a priori* emotional value."[15] Running along the nerve fibres through the arm and out the pen, a line which may in its own way be as inspired as the sentences it underscores, appears upon the page. From a sentence I once underlined in the gnostic *Gospel of Thomas* I have learned to call this illuminating power gnosis: "When you see your image, you are glad. But when you see your images which

---

[12] Hillman, *Archetypal Psychology*, p. 30.
[13] Hillman, *Archetypal Psychology*, p. 30.
[14] Hillman, *Archetypal Psychology*, p. 30.
[15] C. G. Jung, *CW* 6 § 791.

came into being before you, which neither die nor are made, how much will you then endure!"[16]

Reading the works of Freud and Jung alongside the images from Norse mythology "which came into being before them" is both a rich affective experience and a visionary feast. For instance, in connection to the image of Óðinn hung on the windy tree,[17] one finds that the "little vesicle" of emergent life, described by Freud in *Beyond the Pleasure Principle* as being suspended amidst the perturbing stimuli of the world, immediately flashes to mind.[18] Sacrificed to himself in a shamanic rite, the shrieking god is said to have picked up the runes of his wisdom, even as the little vesicle of Freud's speculations, traumatized by the exigencies of nature, develops a protective surface boundary which functions, at the same time, as a consciousness-creating and knowledge-constituting perceptual threshold. Brünnhilde, the battle maiden, lying in the circle of flames bedecked in manly armour, evokes herself, in a like fashion, in those details of Freud's account having to do with how the external stimulation causes the protective surface boundary, or crust of dead matter, to be formed around the vesicle's deeper, living layers.[19] And then there are the resonances from Jung's writings. While underlining those lines of the *Hávamál* which refer to Óðinn's torment upon the tree, Jung's essay, "Mind and Earth," comes forcefully into one's thoughts. For in

---

[16] Cited in Stephen Hoeller, *Jung and the Lost Gospels: Insights into the Dead Sea Scrolls and the Nag Hammadi Library* (Wheaton, IL: The Theosophical Publishing House, 1989), p. 198.

[17] Cf. the *Hávamál* of the *Elder Edda*, stanzas 137, 138.

> I know that I hung
> On that wind-swept tree,
> Through nine long nights,
> Pierced by the spear,
> to Óðinn sacrificed,
> myself to myself,
> on that great tree
> whose roots
> no one knows.
>
> Neither food nor drink
> Did they give me.
> I looked downwards—
> Took up the runes,
> Took them up shrieking,
> Then I fell down.

[18] Sigmund Freud, *Beyond the Pleasure Principle*, tr. J. Strachey (New York: W. W. Norton, 1961), pp. 20-21.

[19] Freud, *Beyond the Pleasure Principle*, pp. 20-21.

*Óðinn sacrificing himself on the World Tree, Yggdrasill, and the
emergence of the runes*

this essay, Jung, too, speculates on the relationship between the psyche and the inorganic world from which it can be conceived to have emerged during the course of evolution. Imagining a descent through historical layers of civilization, Jung would have us reach "the naked bed-rock, and with it that prehistoric time when reindeer hunters fought for a bare and wretched existence against the elemental forces of wild nature."[20] It is within these "dark confines of the earth" that we come upon "the factors that affected us most closely [and which, therefore,] became archetypes" for Jung,[21] even as they became runes for Óðinn.

Although depth psychology from Freud to Hillman has tended to turn to Greek mythology for its ultimate figures, it is useful, in light of this nexus of associations in which the gnosis of the North reveals itself, to explore the extent to which its mode of thought is governed by the frost-demons, boulder-giants, Valkyries, and Rhine-maidens of its own Central and North European landscape.[22] This is not to say that our psychological tradition could not be insighted from other mythological perspectives. In the same way that a dream may take us to a distant land in search of perspectives compensatory to our local psychology, so the

---

[20] Jung, *CW* 10 § 55.
[21] Jung, *CW* 10 § 55.
[22] Cf. Richard Noll, *The Jung Cult: Origins of a Charismatic Movement* (Princeton, N.J.: Princeton University Press, 1994), pp. 92-193. As Noll has shown, the nineteenth century concept of *Bodenbeschaffenheit*—"the formative forces of the soil"—was still current in Jung's day, Jung's friend Count Keyserling, at whose behest Jung wrote his essay "Mind and Earth," being among its most vocal proponents. Supported by the theories of the evolutionary biology of his day, Jung took the formative influence of the landscape more literally, perhaps, than I do in returning to this notion here. For me, outer landscapes reverberate with our interior depths as well as having soul themselves, as Hillman has helped us to better appreciate with his work on *anima mundi*. Thus, it is not necessary to derive materialistically the psyche from the soil, the mind from the earth, but only to note that the experience which the landscape evokes in us cannot be divided into its geology, biology, evolutionary history, etc., without remainder. This remainder, though itself irrepresentable, can, nevertheless, be symbolized by the outer forms which amplify it. Like the synonyms of the philosopher's stone in alchemy, the objective psyche—Jung's term for what I have here referred to as the remainder—reverberates the depths of its subtle nature in the outward forms of actual nature—mountains, lakes, planets and stars. Keyserling recognized this when he wrote that "for the man who believes in myths there are no facts in our sense; he knows nothing of the sun of the physicist [but] prays before what he *feels* as the immediate source of life" (cited in Noll, *The Jung Cult*, p. 94, italics mine). For Jung, too, the archetypal world is not a copy of the external world which science progressively reveals to us. On the contrary, it is a record of the psyche's unconscious reactions to the objects of external reality. See C. G. Jung, *Analytical Psychology: Notes of the Seminar given in 1925*, ed. William McGuire (Princeton, N.J.: Princeton University Press, 1989), pp. 135-136.

various schools of analysis may find compensation through the medium of the so-called "multicultural imagination."²³ In this connection, it is helpful to recall the modesty with which Jung tempered the application of his otherwise bold concept of the collective unconscious. In his "Psychological Commentary to the *Secret of the Golden Flower*," a treatise on Chinese alchemy of some antiquity, Jung writes that our "growing acquaintance with the spiritual East should be no more to us than the symbolical expression of the fact that we are entering into connection with the elements in ourselves which are strange to us."²⁴ Applied to the Northern perspective which we shall be entertaining in this study, perhaps the most that can be said is that Norse mythology resonates with elements in ourselves which are somewhat more familiar.

In each of the chapters that follow, we shall explore Jung's characterization of psychology as a modern mythologem from the vantage point of a different image from Norse myth. In the first chapter, Thor's thunderbolt, the throwing hammer Mjöllnir, will govern our selection and guide our reading of the texts of Freud and Jung. By means of this image, we shall discuss how the *concreteness* of the imaginal and the *impact* of psyche's expressions have been conceptually figured by Freud and Jung in the mythos of their theories. Besides being concrete and impactful, images—and concepts, too, when entertained as images—are life-giving. In the second chapter, this life-giving quality will be explored through the perspective of the sword that Óðinn plunged into the trunk of the Northern oak, Barnstock, at the wedding of Volsung's daughter, Signy. As we shall see, there are many resonances between this Northern saga and the saga that was enacted by Freud, Jung, and Sabina Spielrein in the early days of psychoanalysis. Finally, in the last chapter, the relationship of the imaginal psyche to death and the ancestral dead will be explored alongside such psychological notions as the principle of constancy, the ego-ideal, archetypes and the mana-personality. In this case, our lens is provided by the myth of Baldr.

We began with the image of Óðinn's sacrifice of his eye for the gift of wisdom. A moment ago we mentioned another source of that god's

---

²³ Michael V. Adams, *The Multicultural Imagination: "Race," Color, and the Unconscious* (London: Routledge, 1996).

²⁴ C. G. Jung, "Commentary" to Richard Wilhelm, tr., *The Secret of the Golden Flower: A Chinese Books of Life* (London: Routledge & Kegan Paul, 1962), p. 128. See also C. G. Jung, *CW* 13 § 72.

wisdom: the oracular runes. Exposed to the elements of the ancient north, "the High one" as Óðinn was called, drew what came to be known as the runes from the inwardness and depth of his situation.[25] Closer to our own time, Jung, with a similar dynamic in mind, wrote of the "fantasy combinations" that are latent in the unconscious and which come to light as the press of one's times and conditions bring about their inner constellation.[26] Used in divination, the runes were little pieces of stone, clay, or bark with an alphabet of primitive symbols etched into them. As destiny and fate play at Scrabble through our lives, so the runic fantasy combinations of the imaginal psyche are cast within us by the sympathy and adversity of things, if only in the form of our underlinings, marginal comments, and moments of reverie. Turning now to the texts of Freud and Jung, the task before us is to read them as our forebears read the runes, letting particular passages spring to mind, along with the tales of the North which they continue, from within the press of life and the demands of daily practice.

---

[25] See note 17 above.
[26] Jung, *CW* 8 § 132.

CHAPTER ONE

Thor's Hammer: The Reality and Objectivity of the Psyche in the Thought of Freud and Jung

Thor in his thunder chariot preparing to hurl his throwing hammer, Mjöllnir

The psyche for me is something objective that sends up effects into my consciousness. The unconscious (the *objective psyche*) doesn't belong to me; rightly or wrongly I belong to it. By making it conscious I separate myself from it, and by so objectivating it I can integrate it consciously. Thus my personality is made complete and is prepared for the decisive experience, but no more than that. What can, but need not, happen then is the spontaneous action from the unconscious, an action which is symbolized by the alchemists, Paracelsus, Boehme and the modern unconscious as *lightning*.

—C. G. Jung, *Letters*, vol. II, p. 57.

... [T]he ego is that part of the id which has been modified by the direct influence of the external world ...; in a sense it is an extension of the surface-differentiation. Moreover, the ego seeks to bring the influence of the external world to bear upon the id and its tendencies, and endeavours to substitute the reality principle for the pleasure principle which reigns unrestrictedly in the id. For the ego, perception plays the part which in the id falls to instinct. The ego represents what may be called reason and common sense, in contrast to the id, which contains the passions.

—Sigmund Freud, *The Ego and the Id*, p. 1`5.

God of Lightning

We have already met Thor in the introduction to this volume. As thunder god and lord of the lightning bolt, the fiery, hammer-wielding Thor can be imagined to be the sender of that "bolt from the blue" which compels the psychologically-minded reader to underline those passages in the works of Freud, Jung, and the Norse myths that resonate most thunderously within the associative heart and mind. Though not himself a god of inspiration or revelation, as a son of Óðinn—the Æsir deity to whom these qualities are attached—Thor presents the *power* and *force* of their impact. Just as our Northern forebears compared the rock-smashing, tree-shattering impact of lightning to the spark born of the bronzesmith's hammer, so inspiration strikes us a reverberating blow. We hit upon an insight while reading the Norse myths alongside the writings of Freud and Jung, the mind galvanized by the experience. Ideas come together with a thundering crash. Images hammer us with the imaginal power inherent in them. Even when the mythological image of Thor is the farthest thing from our mind, being altogether unknown to us, it nevertheless remains a possibility of any fantasy, "the archetype," as Hillman has said, being "wholly immanent in its image."[1]

As Thor hurls his throwing hammer, Mjöllnir (the crusher or striker), at the giants and monsters who are the adversaries of the Æsir and their realm, so, with a similar might, the objective psyche throws up images. This is not to say that the objective psyche is any more real than Thor or that the lightning-like force of the one is any more primary than the lightning-like force of the other. Psychology's phrase—"the objective psyche throws up images"—is as mythical a statement as the Norse account of Thor and his throwing hammer. Indeed, we can just as readily see the term "objective psyche" as a shaft of lightning hurled by Thor as we can conceive of Thor's hammer as a mythic image thrown up by the objective psyche.

This is not only true for the mind, but true to experience as well. When one encounters a conceptual term such as "objective psyche" in a text by Jung or a term such as "psychical reality" in an essay of Freud's, one may be struck by an afflux of emotion no less than when one reads about Thor and his hammer. Strangely, despite their abstractness, these concepts have a highly evocative power. While we think of them as ideas, they resound with something deeper, for they are at the same time feelings. The archetype, evidently, is just as immanent to concepts as it is to images. Like a lightning shower, this phenomenon continues to repeat itself in the very words one might draw upon to explain it. In words such as "numinous" and in phrases such as "*a priori* emotional value,"[2] that "spontaneous action from the unconscious ... which is symbolized

---

[1] James Hillman, "On the Necessity of Abnormal Psychology: Ananke and Athene," in J. Hillman, ed. *Facing the Gods* (Irving, TX.: Spring Publications, 1980), p. 10.

[2] C. G. Jung, *Collected Works*, tr. R. F. C. Hull (Princeton, NJ: Princeton University Press, 1953), vol. 6, para. 791. All subsequent references to the *Collected Works* (*CW*), vols. 1-20, will be by volume and paragraph number (designated by §).

by the ... modern unconscious as *lightning*" brings the hammer of Thor to bear once again. In this connection, the following reflection of Jung's seems particularly apt:

> Not for a moment dare we succumb to the illusion that an archetype can be finally explained and disposed of. Even the best attempts at explanation are only more or less successful translations into another metaphorical language. (Indeed, language itself is only an image.) The most we can do is to *dream the myth onwards* and give it a modern dress.[3]

God of Mud

Besides the hammer-like quality of his lightning, another aspect of Thor is evident in these pages: Thor is a warrior god, the defender of the Æsir and their realm from the Jötunns (giants) and other adversaries, such as the monstrous Midgard Serpent. Most of the tales in which he figures celebrate his enormous strength, and the strength of the various opponents over whom he sometime handily, sometimes narrowly prevails. As might be expected, however, his brains do not come up to the same level as his brawn. This is particularly evident when it comes to word-duels. In debates, the obtuse Thor is easily sundered. In contrast to the other gods, who ride over the Rainbow Bridge, Bivrost, to the World Tree, Yggdrasill, where they hold council, Thor takes a less glorious route, plodding on foot through the deep rivers which stream from its base. When the council meeting begins, his performance is consistent with the wretchedness of his entrance. As one commentator describes it,

> He plunges in blindly, but is not wise enough, he blunders and gets completely stuck. He can be so angry that it seems as though fire is flashing from his eyes. He is always busy, and has little time.[4]

When Jung was writing his book, *Psychological Types*, he too became simultaneously bogged down in the enormity of his undertaking and inspired by an image that was thrown up by the unconscious (or by the

---

[3] Jung, *CW* 9, i § 271.
[4] Harald Hveberg, *Of Gods and Giants: Norse Mythology*, tr. P. S. Iversen (Oslo: Johan Grundt Tanum Forlag, 1969), pp 19-20.

lightning bolt of Thor) in response to this situation. As von Franz recounts this story,

> [Dr. Jung had] wanted to write in a clear, logically accurate form, having in mind something like *Le Discours de la Méthode* by Descartes, but he couldn't do it because that was too refined a mental instrument to grasp this enormous wealth of material. When he arrived at this difficulty he dreamt that there was an enormous boat out in the harbour laden with marvellous goods for mankind and that it should be pulled into the harbour and the goods distributed to the people. Attached to this enormous boat was a very elegant, white Arab horse, a beautiful and delicate, highstrung animal which was supposed to pull the ship into harbour. But the horse was absolutely incapable of this. At that moment an enormous red-headed, red-bearded giant came through the mass of people, pushed everybody aside, took an axe, killed the white horse and then took the rope and pulled the whole ship into harbour in one *élan*. So Jung saw that he had to write in the emotional fire he felt about the whole thing and not go on with this elegant white horse. He was then driven by a tremendous working impulse, or emotion, and he wrote the whole book in practically one stretch, getting up every morning at three a.m.[5]

Though Jung identified this red-bearded, axe-wielding figure who is able to free the ship of his writing from the mud in which it had run aground to be a giant, it might be more accurate, in light of our discussion so far, to see this dream as an epiphany of Thor. Like Thor, who is said to appear whenever there is a giant to be faced, this figure, along with the features we have just mentioned, also has the association with elocution discussed above and was a god of seafarers.[6] Jung's account of his dream and the Norse account of Thor evidently tell similar stories of the way things happen. Just as Thor trudges through the muddy river to the council chambers of the gods to make his speeches, so Jung dreamt of a stuck ship and an axe-toting giant or god when he was struggling to articulate himself in his book on types.

---

[5] Marie-Louise von Franz, *The Shadow and Evil in Fairytales* (Zürich: Spring Publications, 1974), p. 209-210.
[6] Thor's association with seafaring derives from the story of his fishing for the Midgard Serpent. For an account of this adventure see Hveberg, *Of Gods and Giants*, pp. 52-54.

In this connection, we may recall Jung's use of the image of a riverbed in his characterization of the archetype as well as a reference in which he relates the "impact" that archetypes have to the act of speech. In the first of these references, Jung describes the archetype as "a deeply graven river-bed in the psyche, in which the waters of life, instead of flowing along as before in a broad but shallow stream, suddenly swell into a mighty river."[7] If in this passage Thor enacts his journey to the council chambers of the Æsir, in the second passage he takes to the podium to deliver his speech:

> The impact of an archetype, whether it takes the form of immediate experience or is expressed through the spoken word, stirs us because it summons up a voice that is stronger than our own. Whoever speaks in primordial images speaks with a thousand voices; he enthrals and overpowers, while at the same time he lifts the idea he is seeking to express out of the occasional and the transitory into the realm of the ever-enduring.[8]

Thor's Hammer in the Thought of Freud and Jung

Psychoanalysis and analytical psychology each present a very different vision of the mud through which Thor of the laboured speech plods to Yggdrasill and the council of the gods. In Freud's writings, these images from Norse mythology find their conceptual equivalents in notions such as infantile sexuality, fixation, and sublimation. Enacting itself in these terms, the mythical mud in which Thor gets stuck corresponds to infantile sexuality's regressive hold, his powerful throwing hammer Mjöllnir, to sexuality itself. The Rainbow Bridge and the council chambers in the branches of the World Ash, Yggdrasill, correspond, by contrast, to the cultural uses to which libido can be applied, providing that infantile forms of gratification can be renounced and their regressive longings sublimated. And herein lies the difficulty, at least in the psychoanalytic version of the story. Pulled in two directions at once, the ambivalent Thor must struggle to free himself from the instinctual vicissitudes in which he is stuck on his way to Yggdrasill, even as the Moses of Michelangelo, in

---

[7] Jung, *CW* 15 § 127.
[8] Jung, *CW* 15 § 129.

Freud's view,[9] was torn between a regressive desire to join the dance around the golden calf and the commandments of his ego-ideal to seek gratification in higher cultural forms. Wrenching a foot free from that viscous muck and then setting it down again while he struggles to free the other, Thor, or rather, the particular instinct or part-drive which is fixated in the muddy embrace of its respective erogenous zone, undergoes what Freud, with the so-called "vicissitudes of the instincts" in mind, has called a "reversal into its opposite."[10] The active stance changes into a passive one, even as in the Norse myth the mighty Thor slumps for a moment in the place where he is stuck. To regain the balance, there is "a reversal of content,"[11] the valence of erotic life shifting from love to hate: heated with frustration, the god gives vent to thunderous rages. Subsequent steps bring about still other instinctual vicissitudes such as "turning around upon the subject," "repression" and "sublimation."[12] Simultaneously sequestered in the primary process which is the corollary, at the mental level, of the part-drives, speech and thought become a muddled affair as well. Though the patient is obliged to say whatever comes into his mind, his associations, as psychoanalysis has long recognized, are anything but free. For just as defences against the instincts oppose the straightforward pursuit of instinctual aims,[13] so resistances oppose compliance with the fundamental rule.[14] Words fail, topics are abruptly changed, and the discourse becomes inexplicably bogged down and blocked. When the patient does seem to be speaking freely, as often as not, it is with the muddy foot of Thor in his mouth— language being redolent of the mechanisms of infantile sexual life that we have just listed. But with an ear for dirt, which is to say, with a knowledge of such muddy mechanisms as displacement, condensation, and symbolization, the analyst listens for the latent meaning of the patient's utterances, formulating them into cogent interpretations which bring the light of reason and reality to bear.

[9] Sigmund Freud, "The Moses of Michelangelo," *Collected Papers*, vol. III: 293-383, tr. J. Riviere (London: The Hogarth Press & The Institute of Psycho-Analysis, 1950). (All subsequent references to the *Collected Papers*—hereafter *CP*—will be by volume and page number.)
[10] Freud, *CP* IV, 69.
[11] Freud, *CP* IV, 69.
[12] Freud, *CP* IV, 69.
[13] Freud, *CP* IV, 69.
[14] Sigmund Freud, *Beyond the Pleasure Principle*, tr. James Strachey (New York: Norton, 1961), pp. 12-14.

From a Jungian perspective, the muddy riverbeds beneath the Rainbow Bridge and the lofty council chamber in the branches of Yggdrasill are not the clear-cut developmental and moral opposites that the Freudian view would suggest. On the contrary, it is as the ends of a continuum, which may be encountered in any image, from the most mundane to the most sublime, that this motif enacts itself in analytical psychology's theories of an objective psyche. Unlike Freud, who championed the light of the rational intellect (that inner representation of the reality principle) over the darkly infantile fantasies which the pleasure principle perversely spawns, Jung, like Paracelsus before him, conceives the muddy images in which our lives are mired to be suffused from the outset with the *a priori* consciousness of an archetypal light.[15] Like the treasure troves and gold mines of the Northern dwarves and elves which lie hidden under boulders and beneath the roots of trees, the *lumen naturae,* or natural light, is trapped, as is the celestial *nous* of gnostic speculation, in the heaviness of matter itself.

It is not only that the archetype is wholly immanent in its image, as we have already heard from Hillman. Nor is it that matter and spirit, like the mud and lightning in our Northern myth, coalesce in what has been called an intermediary world of images.[16] To these axioms, a third one, adapted from an adage of Edward Casey's,[17] must be added if we are to fully declare the mud in the eye of a fully imaginal perspective: *an image is not what we see, but how we see and are seen from the transpersonal perspective of the objective psyche.*[18]

---

[15] Jung, *CW* 8 § 387-396.

[16] Cf. my "The Between-ness of Things: Psyche as the Intermediary between Matter and Spirit," *Harvest: International Journal for Jungian Studies* 50:1 (2004).

[17] "An image is not *what* we see, but *how* we see." Adage adapted from his statement: "The image is not *what* is present to awareness—this is the content proper—but *how* this content is presented." Edward S. Casey, "Toward a Phenomenology of Imagination," *Journal of the British Society for Phenomenology* 5 (1974): 10.

[18] To Casey's adage, cited in the previous note, I have added the notion of being known by an unknown knower. Of this Edinger writes: "The experience of knowing with can be understood to mean the ability to participate in a knowing process simultaneously as subject and object, the knower and the known. This is only possible within a relationship to an object that can also be a subject. Practically, this means either a relationship with an outer other (a person) or an inner other (the Self)." Edward Edinger, *The Creation of Consciousness: Jung's Myth for Modern Man* (Toronto: Inner City Books, 1984), p. 53. We shall return to this theme in the final chapter, discussing it there in terms of our relationship to the ancestral soul.

Though the intellect, given to abstraction, may conceive of the archetypal psyche as a realm of isolated and cleanly differentiated monads, the archetypes, writes Jung, exist "in a state of contamination of the most complete mutual interpenetration and interfusion."[19] Mixed up with one another in this undifferentiated state, the various archetypal faces of the collective unconscious become clear to us only when we are as mired in one or another of the sink holes of life as they are in each other. As Jung puts it, "When a situation occurs which corresponds to a given archetype, that archetype become activated and a compulsiveness appears, which, like an instinctual drive, gains its way against all reason and will, or else produces a conflict of pathological dimensions, that is to say, a neurosis."[20]

Freud, of course, could not credit such a view. Though he, too, was immensely interested in the psyche's primordial reaches, the tendency to attribute wisdom to them was anathema to him.[21] Myth and religion, in his view, were a primeval slime redolent of mankind's most infantile urges—early man standing in the same relationship to his contemporary counterpart, neurotic man, as the perverse nursling stands in relation to the mature adult. The best that could be said of them was that their motifs and creeds bore witness to the transformation, via renunciation and sublimation, of the blind impulsiveness of the id into the imperatives of the ego-ideal:

> The ego ideal is ... the heir of the Oedipus complex, and
> thus it is also the expression of the most powerful impulses
> and most important libidinal vicissitudes of the id. By setting
> up this ego ideal, the ego has mastered the Oedipus complex
> and at the same time placed itself in subjection to the id.
> Whereas the ego is essentially the representative of the
> external world, of reality, the super-ego stands in contrast
> to it as the representative of the internal world, of the id.

---

[19] C. G. Jung, *The Integration of the Personality*, tr. S. Dell (London: Kegan & Paul, 1940), p. 91. See also Jung, *CW* 9, i § 302— "It is a well-nigh hopeless undertaking to tear a single archetype out of the living tissue of the psyche; but despite their interwovenness they do form units of meaning that can be apprehended intuitively."

[20] Jung, *CW* 9, i § 99.

[21] For a remarkable reading of Freud's super-ego theory that shows that it is compatible with the idea of a wise unconscious see Dan Merkur, *Unconscious Wisdom: A Superego Function in Dreams, Conscience, and Inspiration* (Albany: State University of New York, 2001).

> Conflicts between the ego and the ideal will, as we are now
> prepared to find, ultimately reflect the contrast between what
> is real and what is psychical, between the external world and
> the internal world.[22]

While with this theory, Freud certainly does meet the reproach of those
critics who had complained that psychoanalysis ignores "the higher,
moral, supra-personal side of human nature,"[23] the tale it tells is a most
pessimistic one given that the super-ego, which has developed as the result
of this same process, is regarded as casting such long shadows of
discontent upon the future.[24]

Against Freud's anxious admonishment that he cleave dogmatically
to the sexual theories of psychoanalysis and make an "unshakable
bulwark" of them "against the black tide of mud ... of occultism"[25] that
his own emerging theories threatened to release Jung held fast. For to
him Freud's position, taken to its ultimate conclusion, would "lead to
an annihilating judgement upon culture," culture appearing on this
account to be "a mere farce, the morbid consequence of repressed
sexuality."[26] Having immersed himself to the knees, and higher, in his
mythological researches, Jung came to believe that the mind's mythical
substrate was not the mere quagmire of repressed material that Freud
believed it to be at that time,[27] but a reservoir of vitality, resilience, and
proto-adaptive tendencies. As with Thor, however, it was at first painfully
difficult for him to articulate his ideas to Freud, derived as they were
from the very fantasy thinking that he, like Freud, had until that point

---

[22] Sigmund Freud, *The Ego and the Id*, ed, J. Strachey, tr. J. Riviere (New York:
W. W. Norton, 1962), p. 26.

[23] Freud, *The Ego and the Id*, p. 25.

[24] Sigmund Freud, *Civilization and its Discontents*, in *The Freud Pelican Library*,
vol. 12: 251-340 (Harmondsworth: Penguin Books, 1985).

[25] C. G. Jung, *Memories, Dreams, Reflections*, tr. R. & C. Winston (New York:
Random House, 1965), p. 150.

[26] Jung, *Memories, Dreams, Reflections*, p. 150.

[27] Though Jung tended to characterize Freud's view of the unconscious as limited
to the repressed, and though I have here limited my amplification of the mud in which
Thor mucks to Freud's notions of repression, fixation and infantile sexuality, Freud
clearly recognized that the unconscious comprised much more than repressed contents.
In *The Ego and the Id*, Freud speaks of a structure in the ego which, while providing
for consciousness, has itself never been conscious. Conceptualizing this region of the
mind as the "third unconscious," Freud maps something of the same territory Jung
mapped with his notion of a psychoid unconscious. Discussion of these ideas, however,
I will leave to the final chapter, for they do not have the muddy quality which concerns
us here, being rather more rigid, inorganic, and stone-like.

regarded with suspicion.[28] It was a very troubled Jung who would write
to his patient and confidant, Sabina Spielrein, "I have been blasphemed
enough, mocked enough, and criticized thoroughly; therefore I will keep
my runes and all my pale and thin little ideas, some of which I shared
in my 'Libido' work," even though, as he bitterly added, "[they are only]
'unscientific,' symbolic lies built on repressed anal eroticism."[29] Evidently,
at this point in his career, Jung only dimly perceived what he would
later, with the help of his alchemical research, see more clearly: lightning
and mud constellate together even as the gold (as the adage puts it) is
in the shit.

Jung's later conviction "that creative imagination is the only
primordial phenomenon accessible to us, the real Ground of the psyche"[30]
began to take hold in him with the recognition that it was the *mythical*
power of Freud's sexual theory,[31] not sexuality itself, that exerted the
fascinating, not to say fixating, effect which Freud attributed to libido.
As the only immediate reality accessible to us, images, in Jung's view,[32]
are more indicative of our psychic nature than is sexuality. They, not
sexuality, are the mud in which we plod, even as they, not sexuality, are
the source of the lightning which enlivens our being.

Where the unconsciously mythical language of Freud's psychoanalysis
would assimilate the image of the muddy Thor to its psycho-sexual theory
of regression and fixation, the more consciously mythical language of
Jung's analytical psychology would speak of a potentially positive
introversion of psychic interest into the depths of its own symbolical
imagery. As Jung put it in the later, revised edition of the chapter of his
Wandlungen und Symbole der Libido, which, in its original version,
signalled the end of his collegial relations with Freud:

[28] C. G. Jung, *Analytical Psychology: Notes of the Seminar given in 1925*, ed. W.
McGuire (Princeton, N.J.: Princeton University Press, 1989), pp. 27-28.
[29] Cited in John Kerr, *A Most Dangerous Method: The Story of Jung, Freud, and
Sabina Spielrein* (New York: Alfred A. Knopf, 1993), p. 482.
[30] C. G. Jung, *Letters*, vol. I: 1906-1950 & vol. II: 1951-1961, ed. G. Adler & A. Jaffé,
tr. R. F. C. Hull (Princeton, NJ: Princeton University Press, 1973 & 1975), vol. I, p. 60.
[31] Cf. Jung, *Memories, Dreams, Reflections*, p. 151: "Freud, who had always made
much of his irreligiosity, had ... in the place of a jealous God whom he [as a self-
proclaimed "godless Jew"] had lost, ... substituted another compelling image, that of
sexuality. It was no less insistent, exacting, domineering, threatening, and morally
ambivalent than the original one. Just as the psychically stronger agency is given 'divine'
or 'daemonic' attributes, so the 'sexual libido' took over the role of a *deus absconditus*,
a hidden or concealed god."
[32] Jung, *CW* 8 § 680.

The regressing libido apparently desexualizes itself by retreating back step by step to the presexual stage of earliest infancy. Even there it does not make a halt, but in a manner of speaking continues right back to the intra-uterine, pre-natal condition and, leaving the sphere of personal psychology altogether, irrupts into the collective psyche .... The libido thus reaches a kind of inchoate condition in which, like Theseus and Peirithous on their journey to the underworld, it may easily stick fast. But it can also tear itself loose from the maternal embrace and return to the surface with new possibilities of life.[33]

This view of the mud, which was as much the product of Jung's Thor-like return to his childhood pursuit of making rivulets for his fantasies in the shoreline of Lake Zürich as it was the result of his scholarly research into the nature of myth,[34] is indeed a radical departure from the views of Freud. From this perspective, both the mud of myth and the stuff of theory are essential expressions of the psyche's symbolic process.

The symbolic process is an experience *in images and of images.* Its development usually shows an enantiodromian structure ... a rhythm of negative and positive, loss and gain, dark and light. *Its beginning is almost invariably characterized by one's getting stuck in a blind alley or in some impossible situation; and its goal is, broadly speaking, illumination or higher consciousness, by means of which the initial situation is overcome on a higher level.*[35]

Just as eternity can be glimpsed in a grain of sand, and Thor in a debate over theory, the objective psyche, that mythological mud of interpenetrating archetypes, is illuminatingly present in the images and ideas to which we are subject wherever we are stuck. It does not matter whether we have come to a halt in one of the great transitional periods of our lives or are simply bogged down in a creative project (as Jung was when he was writing his *Psychological Types*), sooner or later the lightning-hurling, rune-casting psyche will react with an image or fantasy which

---

[33] Jung, *CW* 5 § 654.
[34] Deirdre Bair, *Jung: A Biography* (Boston: Little, Brown & Company, 2003, p. 245.) See also Jung, *Memories, Dreams, Reflections*, pp. 173-175.
[35] Jung, *CW* 9, I § 82. Italics mine.

Thor in Útgarða-Loki's castle

"bridge[s] the irreconcilable claims of subject and object"[36] such that life can carry on. God (or that imago of the psyche which so transcends the boundaries of the ego that we experience it as if it were a deity) really does hear the sparrow fall, in one situation becoming Thor to do so, in other situations taking on the form of still other gods—hence Jung's hypothesis of a collective unconscious.[37]

Thor, Jung, and Freud in Útgarða-Loki's Castle

> What we can safely say about mythical images is that the physical process imprinted itself on the psyche in this fantastic, distorted form and was preserved there, so that the unconscious still reproduces similar images today. Naturally the question now arises: why does the psyche not register the actual process, instead of mere fantasies about the physical process?[38]
>
> —C. G. Jung

Our reference above to the lightning-hurling, rune-casting psyche raises important questions. How, we must now ask, is it that the psyche is so constituted? And what account do the stories of Thor, reiterated in the theories of psychoanalysis and analytical psychology, give of how the so-called objective inner world of the psyche has come into being?

In the "elder edda"[39] of psychoanalysis, legends like those in the Norse cycle depicting Thor as the matchless adversary of the Jötunns are told. Where the Norse myths speak of frost-giants and boulder-demons, however, Freud's myth speaks of the id-modifying "influence of the external world."[40] And where the Norse account describes Thor

---

[36] Jung, *CW* 6 § 78.

[37] In using the term "collective unconscious" interchangeably with the term "God" I follow Jung's precedent: "For the collective unconscious we could use the word God. ... [But] I prefer not to use big words, I am quite satisfied with humble scientific language because it has the great advantage of bringing the whole experience into our immediate vicinity." C. G. Jung, *The Visions Seminars* (Zürich: Spring Publications, 1976), p. 391.

[38] Jung, *CW* 8 § 328.

[39] The "Poetic" or "Elder Edda" is a compilation of mythic tales and poems. Dating from 1250 C.E., it is also referred to as Saemund's Edda after a famous Icelander. The "Younger Edda," also called the "Prose Edda," is a later compilation written by Snorri Sturluson around 1220 C.E.

[40] Freud, *The Ego and Id*, p. 7.

as appearing whenever called upon for aid against the Jötunns and the Vanir, Freud conceptualizes a psychic agency of similar characteristics, the "I" or "ego," which is called into being through the clash between the instinctual impulses of the id and the forces at large in the surrounding environment.

The "younger edda" of Jung's analytical psychology tells much the same story. Indeed, like Freud, Jung also conceives of an ego which, as he puts it, "seems to arise in the first place from the collision between the somatic factor and the environment, and once established as a subject, ... goes on developing from further collisions with the outer world and the inner."[41]

The tale of Thor's encounters with the Jötunn, Skryme, and Útgarða-Loki, the King of the Jötunns,[42] comes immediately to mind in connection with Freud's and Jung's accounts of the clash or collision of the somatic factor, or id, with the external world.

Awakened in the night by a ground-trembling earthquake, Thor and his companions discover an enormous giant sleeping nearby. So enormous is this giant that it is by his snoring that the earth has been made to quake. Upon awakening the giant introduces himself to Thor. His name is Skryme. As mighty as Thor is, he is clearly minuscule compared to this Jötunn. As Skryme rises to dress, Thor realizes that what he had thought to be a house and had taken shelter in for the night was in fact merely the thumb of the giant's glove! Doubtless, the sheer immensity of Skryme accounts for Thor's accepting his invitation that they travel together. The friendly relations that seem to have been established between these sworn enemies, however, is more apparent than real. While Thor allows himself to be carried along by the great strides of his new companion (and we humans do as well when we are overwhelmed by a new stimulus), his "identification with the aggressor"[43] is short-lived. At nightfall, after finding that he is unable to muster sufficient strength to open the sack of provisions that Skryme had hospitably offered to him before retiring for the night, Thor undertakes to add the sleeping giant to his long list of slain Jötunns. Taking up his hammer, Mjöllnir, the thunder god approaches Skryme of the thunderous snores, striking the

---

[41] Jung, *CW* 9ii § 6.
[42] My telling of this tale follows the account of Hveberg, *Of Gods and Giants*, pp. 41-51.
[43] Anna Freud, *The Ego and the Mechanisms of Defense*, tr. C. Baines (New York: International Universities Press, 1966), p. 109-121.

sleeping giant on the head. Though we may be sure that the blow was a mighty one, the groggy Skryme merely awakens wondering if it was a leaf that has fallen on his head. Twice more Thor brings his hammer down upon Skryme, the Jötunn thinking that perhaps an acorn or a twig has fallen on him.

Bearing in mind that the mythical events I have just described and the depth psychological concepts which appear to resemble them cannot be explained through reduction to each other's terms, let us briefly re-tell the tale of Thor and Skryme in terms of resembling motifs from the thought of Freud. As the juxtaposition of these motifs renders what is familiar about the one mythology strange and what is strange about the other mythology familiar, something objective in the background of both is thrown vividly into relief, or as Jung would say, amplified.

The Norse account of Thor's having been awakened by the earth-shaking snores of the Jötunn Skyrme is reminiscent of Freud's account of the ego's origins in the clash between the external world and the id, a concept that we have already discussed. Likewise, the story of how Thor subsequently brought his hammer to bear upon the brow of his sleeping foe, only to have his foe mistake that blow for the tickle of a falling leaf, is reminiscent of the repressive tendency that Freud attributed to the ego. In the materialistic view of Freud, the dialectic from which the inner world of psychical reality is built up is the consequence of the id actively turning upon itself, in the form of the ego, a modified version of the collisions with the external world which formed the ego out of the id in the first place. Born of this process, psychic images are neither true copies of external objects, nor wholly transparent to the id and its impulses, but a muddy fusion of the two. Having derived their form and force from the collision between the id and the external world, which they simultaneously seek to repress, these images create, through subsequent collisions of their own with one another,[44] an illusory space or psychical reality of increasingly immense proportions.

---

[44] I refer here to the illuminating comparison of one thing to another, i.e., to the capacity to know what things are *like*, as this comes across in metaphor and simile, image, symbol and myth.

Clearly, Freud's vision of the ego, as simultaneously protecting and propitiating the id by offering it hallucinatory forms of satisfaction, resonate with the hammer blows that Thor dealt to Skryme.[45] For, like that sleeping Jötunn in the Norse myth, the mental apparatus of Freudian theory is constituted in such a way that when it dreams, impinging impressions reaching it from the instincts and the external world are also mistaken for the tickling of a leaf, or whatever other image may emerge to protect our sleep. Similar processes underpin the production of neurotic symptoms as well. Like Skyrme awakened by Thor's hammer-blows and thinking that a leaf, an acorn, and then a twig has fallen upon his head, neurotics, according to Freudian theory, defend themselves from the ultimate sources of their suffering by representing their thoughts, fantasies and symptoms in such a way that they may remain unconscious of their true origin and meaning. Little Hans, to take but one example, protected himself from his dread Oedipal fears by developing a horse phobia.[46] In the case of the traumatic neuroses, on the other hand, the blows of fate cannot be reduced to such trifles as a falling leaf, an acorn, or a twig, although after many thousands of repetitions, the onslaughts of almost unmediated affect-images which characterize these disturbances may also begin to vary their imagery, thereby becoming subject to soul-making.[47]

But for Freud, the mental apparatus does not only distort reality as a means of defence; it also develops the capacity to face it without illusions. While nature may be the first to bring its mighty hammer to bear upon the creatures that dwell in its midst, once subjected to the "thousand natural shocks that mortal flesh is heir to,"[48] that part of the id that has been traumatized to the point where it now bears the image

---

[45] Freud, *The Ego and the Id*, p. 7: "We have formed the idea that in each individual there is a coherent organization of mental processes; and we call this his *ego*. It is to this ego that consciousness is attached; the ego controls the approaches to motility— that is, to the discharge of excitations into the external world; it is the mental agency which supervises all its own constituent processes, and which goes to sleep at night, though even then it exercises the censorship on dreams. From this ego proceed the repressions ...."

[46] Freud, *CP* III: 149-289.

[47] Jung, *CW* 8 § 499-500. Cf. Harry Wilmer, "Combat Nightmares: Toward a Therapy of Violence," *Spring 1986: An Annual of Archetypal Psychology and Jungian Thought* (Dallas: Spring Publications, 1986), pp. 120-139.

[48] William Shakespeare, *Hamlet*, III.i, ll. 63-64.

and likeness of the forces afflicting it comes to wield a hammer of its own. As both the inner representative of the external world and the mental agency which controls the discharge of libidinal excitations into the surrounding environment, the Thor-like "ego seeks to bring the influence of the external world to bear upon the id and its tendencies, and … to substitute the reality principle for the pleasure principle which reigns unrestrictedly in the id."[49] The sparks of light and flashes of lightning that are born of this hammer-like clash of opposing forces correspond, in Freud's account, to the "reason and common sense" that the ego has gleaned (phylogenetically and ontogenetically) from its travail in the school of hard knocks which the world provides.[50]

Before examining the ideas of Jung's that come to mind in connection with this discussion, let us return to our Northern tale.

Awakening the following morning, quite untrammelled by the hammer-blows he received during the night, Skryme invites Thor and his companions to travel with him to the castle of Útgarð, a Jötunn stronghold. There, he wryly informs them, they will meet even bigger fellows than himself. Thor accepts the veiled challenge and agrees to go along. Though his failed attempt to kill Skryme the previous night does not augur well for such a journey, the nature of his divinity is predicated on such against-all-odds encounters. Who, after all, would Thor be without such Jötunn foils?

After a day's travel, Thor and company find themselves at the castle of Útgarð. As castles go, this one is of an extraordinarily immense size. To see the height of it, Thor must bend over backwards. To enter its keep, he must step, mouse-like, through the bars of the door.

Once inside the castle, the visitors find themselves in the looming presence of its resident Jötunns. Útgarða-Loki, the Jötunn King, introduces himself to them. Insulting his guests on account of their relatively small size, he immediately challenges them to compete against his Jötunns in a series of contests and trials of strength.

---

[49] Freud, *The Ego and Id*, p. 7. See epigraph at top of this chapter.

[50] Musical passages from Stravinsky's *Le Sacre du Printemps* come to mind at this juncture as if to remind me that the metapsychological Freud was a visionary Freud and that the technical terms he created denote much more than the mental apparatus of the human subject. Indeed, the simplest life forms at the dawn of creation are subject to the same descriptive categories. As Freud puts it, "The differentiation between ego and id must be attributed not only to primitive man but even to much simpler organisms, for its is the inevitable expression of the influence of the external world" (*The Ego and the Id*, p. 28).

In the first contest, Thor's companion Loki is pitted against the Jötunn Loge in an eating contest. Although Loki eats the great trough of meat laid before him with great speed and gusto, Loge consumes not only the meat, but the bones and trough as well, in the same brief period.

The eating contest

In subsequent contests, Thor's contingent fares no better. After the swift Tjalve loses a foot race against a Jötunn boy named Huge, Thor himself enters the competition. Renowned for his capacity to drink great draughts of ale, the barrel-chested Æsir might have expected to be able to drain the ale-horn which Útgarða-Loki offers him with a few fast gulps. After three attempts, however, Thor finds to his chagrin that the horn is still far from empty. Inviting his bewildered guest to other contests, Útgarða-Loki mockingly suggests that the mighty Thor now see if he can lift the castle cat up off the floor. In this, as well, Thor is defeated. Though he raises the cat very high, the arch of its back is so great that he is only able to raise one of its paws from the floor. And then, adding further insult to Thor's injured pride, Útgarða-Loki suggests a final contest. Would the great Thor test his strength in a wrestling match against the king's elderly foster-mother?! Thor by this time is enraged enough to wrestle anything placed in his path. But here again his efforts prove to be to no avail. Even this old hag puts him to shame with quick dispatch.

With this final and most humiliating defeat, Útgarða-Loki calls off any further contests and invites Thor and his companions to table. Extending to his guests the best of hospitality, Útgarða-Loki then treats them to an enormous feast. Bitterly, Thor and his party eat their meal as if it were a sorry dish of humble pie. After a second feed the following morning, they prepare to leave.

It is at this point, just as Thor and his contingent are about to step through the door and out of the castle, that Útgarða-Loki reveals to his humiliated and shamefaced guests how things really are. From their very

Thor attempting to lift the castle cat off the floor

first encounter, Útgarða-Loki, then in the form of the Jötunn Skryme, has used magic and cunning to protect himself and his fellow Jötunns from the strength of Thor, which he only pretended to hold in small account. As he explains to his incredulous guests, the sack of provisions which he, as Skryme, had given to Thor could not be opened because it was tied with magic yarn. And as for the hammer blows that Thor had aimed at the sleeping Skryme, even the first of these would have killed him had not he, mercurial trickster that he is, pulled a mountain between the hammer and himself. As evidence of this deception, the guests are shown the flattened mountain and the three square valleys that Thor's hammer made in it. And what of the eating contest? Recognizing that Thor's Loki could eat most greedily, Útgarða-Loki had pitted him against a raging fire that could consume the bones and trough as fast as it could the meat. Continuing the litany of deceptions, Útgarða-Loki reveals that the Jötunn, Huge, whom Tjalve had raced, was in fact the memory and thought of their Jötunn host. Tjalve could hardly be expected to outrun these! Then there had been the ale-horn which Thor had attempted to drain. In this event as well Thor's performance had been most impressive, for the other end of the horn lay in the sea. Though because of this the horn could not be emptied, Thor had drunk so deeply from it that his gulps created what is now known as the ebb-tide! And what trickery was involved in the last two contests? What Útgarða-Loki had identified as his cat and challenged Thor to lift off the floor was actually the dread Midgard Serpent, whose length is that of the entire land! The mocking Jötunns were really most astounded that Thor had lifted the arching monster almost to heaven! They were also impressed by Thor's performance in the last contest, for while he was deceived into believing that the old hag with whom he was wrestling was merely Útgarða-Loki's foster-mother, it was actually "Old Age" with whom he was fighting. No one, not even an Æsir deity, can prevail over that spirit!

Upon hearing the full account of these trials and deceptions, Thor quickly took up his hammer, hoping to deal the long-overdue death-blow to his host, but just as quickly, Útgarða-Loki disappeared, his castle vanishing also.

If psychology, as Jung has suggested, is the "[translation] of the archaic speech of myth into a modern mythologem,"[51] what mythologem, we might ask, does Jung's analytical psychology use to re-tell this Northern tale? Or, said another way, in what conceptual terms do Thor, Skryme and Útgarða-Loki enact themselves in Jung's thought?

We have already examined the theories in Freud's thought in which Thor enacts his initial encounter with the enormous Skryme. Turning now to a consideration of Jung's theories, we find that in so doing we follow the plot of our Northern myth. For just as Thor accepted Skryme's invitation to accompany him to the castle of Útgarð, where he would meet Jötunns that were even larger than Skryme himself, so Jung's theories invite us to conceive of the psyche as an immensity in which we are contained, an immensity, moreover, which is replete with giants of its own. These giants, which Jung calls archetypes, are the inner equivalents of the elemental giants of the external environment from which Freud would mechanistically derive the mental apparatus. Though occasionally described by Jung in definitional statements as having evolved in relation to external forces along something of the same lines as Freud describes,[52]

---

[51] Jung, *CW* 9i § 302.
[52] Jung, *CW* 10 § 49-56.

archetypes for Jung also partake of "a causeless and creative principle" which
cannot be entirely derived from material processes.[53]

Quotations from Jung's writings which dream the archaic myth of
Thor's sojourn in Útgarð onwards by translating it into modern dress
are many. Keeping the entire story of Thor's encounter with Skryme and
Útgarða-Loki in mind, let us cite a few of these.

> I can only gaze with wonder and awe at the depths and
> heights of our psychic nature. Its non-spatial universe
> conceals an untold abundance of images which have
> accumulated over millions of years of living development
> and become fixed in the organism. My consciousness is like
> an eye that penetrates to the most distant spaces, yet it is
> the psychic non-ego that fills them with non-spatial images.
> And these images are not pale shadows, but tremendously
> powerful psychic factors. The most we may be able to do is
> misunderstand them, but we can never rob them of their
> power by denying them. Beside this picture I would like to
> place the spectacle of the starry heavens at night, for
> the only equivalent of the universe within is the
> universe without ....[54]

Like Thor, awestruck by the sheer immensity of the castle of Útgarð and
humbled before the Jötunns who defeated him with the aid of Útgarða-
Loki's deceptive magic, Jung speaks in this passage of his numinous
encounter with the depths and heights of a psychic nature constituted
of images which, far from being merely the pale shadows of the external
world, are powerful psychic factors in their own right. Though we, like
Thor, may misunderstand these images, or be deceived by them, we
cannot, writes Jung, rob them of their Æsiric and Jötunnic power by
denying their reality. The fact that they, being non-spatial, appear and
disappear of their own accord, as does Útgarða-Loki's castle in our myth,
points, not to the insubstantiality of images (Freud's theory of images as
mere wish-fulfillment), but to the independence and autonomy of the
psychic factor.[55] For, as Jung writes elsewhere, when the effects that these
images produce are taken into account, their determining influence must
also be acknowledged.

---

[53] Jung, *CW* 10 § 49.
[54] Jung, *CW* 4 § 764.
[55] Jung, *CW* 9, i § 116-118.

Let us now examine another passage from Jung's writings in which Útgarða-Loki's revelation of his true nature to Thor can be overheard:

> "All that is outside, also is inside," we could say with Goethe. But this "inside," which modern rationalism is so eager to derive from "outside," has an *a priori* structure of its own that antedates all conscious experience. It is quite impossible to conceive how "experience" in the widest sense, or, for that matter, anything psychic, could originate exclusively in the outside world. The psyche is part of the inmost mystery of life, and it has its own peculiar structure and form like every other organism. Whether this psychic structure and its elements, the archetypes, ever "originated" at all is a metaphysical question and therefore unanswerable. The structure is something given, the precondition that is found to be present in every case. And this is the *mother*, the matrix—the form into which all experience is poured.[56]

If Thor's hammer in the hand of Freud would aim its blows at Skryme, here in the hand of Jung, as in the previous quotation, it is aimed at that mercurial trickster, Útgarða-Loki. For just as Útgarða-Loki, in the course of exposing his deceptions to Thor, reveals that he had been Thor's companion from the outset, appearing to him earlier than Thor had previously realized in the form of Skryme, so Jung speaks of the psyche as having an "*a priori* structure of its own which antedates all conscious experience." Inasmuch as this structure is always already the precondition of the theoretical fantasies that we would bring to bear upon it, it truly is a metaphysical question whether it ever originated at all. Even theories as brilliant and visionary as those of Freud, far from dealing a devastatingly explicative blow to the psychic problem, fall upon it as a leaf, an acorn, or a twig out of the psyche's own *a priori* nature.

Jung's point about consciousness being antedated by a shaping structure is a crucial one. Indeed, it would be no exaggeration to characterize it as the very cornerstone of his thought. Stated negatively, the *a priori* structure that Jung attributes to the psyche is the empirical corollary of the epistemological conundrum peculiar to psychology, namely, its lack of an Archimedean perspective.[57] Because it is quite without an extrapsychic vantage point, and can therefore never completely

---

[56] Jung, *CW* 9i § 187.
[57] Jung, *CW* 11 § 87.

separate itself as formulating subject from the object its seeks to investigate, psychology finds itself unable to defeat the giants with which it jostles. Its theories are also fantasies, mythologems in modern dress, rooted in archetypes which precede their present formulation even as the myths of our Northern forebears antedate the discoveries of psychoanalysis and analytical psychology. As with Thor, so with psychology: no sooner do we believe that we have struck a mortal blow to Skryme than we find ourselves to have been deceived by Útgarða-Loki.

While psychoanalysis as inaugurated by Freud, like modern rationalism generally, bashes away at Skryme with its mechanistic prejudice that the inner world of the psyche can be derived exclusively from the external world, Jung, in rejecting this view, takes a swipe at the fleeting visage of Útgarða-Loki. Of course, the hammer of Jung's theories, no less than Freud's, whizzes passed its target as he does so. This, however, is less important than Jung's recognition that it always returns, like Thor's Mjöllnir, with consciousness-advancing insights into the psychic structures enveloping it.

The important point here is not simply that the projections contained in our theories, like projections generally, are "always an indirect process of becoming conscious."[58] Given psychology's predicament with respect to its lack of an Archimedean perspective, the process is more circular than that. No sooner have we formulated the consciousness we have gleaned from one projection into the terms of a more embracing theory than we find that we are humbled once again, as were Thor and his party in their contests with the Jötunns, by another projection.[59] When this process is grasped, however, for the symbolical process that it actually is, it can be affirmed as a method of knowing that names the unknown by the name of the more unknown[60]—in Jung's text by such names as collective unconscious, archetype and Mercurius, in these pages by such names as Thor and Útgarða-Loki.

---

[58] Jung, *CW* 14 § 486.

[59] Cf. Marie-Louise von Franz, *Projection and Re-Collection in Jungian Psychology: Reflections of the Soul* (La Salle & London: Open Court, 1980), p. 38: "This seems to correspond to a general psychological law: *The statement of the new truth reveals the previous conceptions as 'projections' and tries to draw them into the psychic inner world, and at the same time it announces a new myth, which now passes for the finally discovered 'absolute' truth.*"

[60] "If [man] possesses a grain of wisdom, he will lay down his arms and name the unknown by the more unknown, *ignotum per ignotius*—that is, by the name of God." Jung, *Memories, Dreams, Reflections*, p. 354.

But let us now examine another passage from Jung's writings, reading it, too, as if it were the speech of Útgarða-Loki revealing his deceits to Freud and Thor:

> It is not storms, not thunder and lightning ... that remain as images in the psyche, but the fantasies caused by the affects they arouse. I once experienced a violent earthquake, and my first, immediate feeling was that I no longer stood on the solid and familiar earth, but on the skin of a gigantic animal that was heaving under my feet. [Note here the lack of an Archimedean point on which to stand!—G. M.]. It was this image that impressed itself on me, not the physical fact. Man's curses against devastating thunderstorms, his terror of the unchained elements—these affects anthropomorphize the passion of nature, and the purely physical element becomes an angry god.
>
> Like the physical condition of his environment, the physiological conditions, glandular secretions, etc., also can arouse fantasies charged with affect. Sexuality appears as a god of fertility ... or as a terrifying serpent that squeezes its victims to death.[61]

Though Jung acknowledged that "myth[s] undoubtedly [contain] a reflection of the physical process [and that, therefore,] many investigators assume that the primitives invent[ed them] merely to explain the physical process,"[62] he also saw them as being structured *a priori* by a psychic factor that is discontinuous with the physical process, though perhaps in synchronistic relationship with it. The earthquake as we have come to know it through seismological instrumentation is not registered as such by the experiencing psyche, but as a gigantic animal heaving underfoot— or a gigantic snoring Jötunn. Our experience of the glandular secretions occurring in our own bodies, likewise, is mediated to us by a world of fantasy images—hence Jung's adage that the "body is as metaphysical as spirit."[63] Even without compelling external stimuli, such as the earthquake and hormones mentioned by Jung, the psyche's images may constellate to huge effect. Molehills become mountains; tempests rage in teapots. Taking particular note of such phenomena, Jung advised that

---

[61] Jung, *CW* 8 § 331-332.
[62] Jung, *CW* 8 § 327.
[63] Jung, *Letters*, vol. I, p. 200.

whenever a "psychic reaction ... is out of proportion to its precipitating cause [it] should be investigated as to whether it may be conditioned at the same time by an archetype."[64]

Thor's Hammer Stolen and Reclaimed

> Innumerable facts prove that the psyche translates physical processes into sequences of images which have hardly any recognizable connection with the objective process. The materialistic hypothesis is much too bold and flies in the face of experience with almost metaphysical presumption. ... There is ... no ground at all for regarding the psyche as something secondary or as an epiphenomenon; on the contrary, there is every reason to regard it, at least hypothetically, as a factor *sui generis*, and to go on doing so until it has been sufficiently proved that the psychic processes can be fabricated in a retort.[65]

The argument which Jung advances here, and in many other places in his writings, against the materialistic hypothesis and its tendency to conceive of the psyche as being something secondary, a mere epiphenomenon, is reminiscent of another tale of Thor from the Norse cycle. By reminding ourselves of this tale we can amplify something of the *a priori* psychic structure that shaped Jung's recognition of the reality of this factor. Where previously we have dreamed the archaic myth along by translating it into the modern mythologem of psychological theory, now we dream the modern mythologem of analytical psychology onward by recasting it in archaic dress—*ignotum per ignotius*.

The tale I am thinking of concerns Thor's regaining of his lost hammer, Mjöllnir. Like the tale of Thor's encounter with Skryme and Útgarða-Loki, this tale also deals with deceptive trickery. This time, however, it is Thor, with the aid of his cunning companion Loki, who plays the trickster.

Awakening one morning, Thor finds that his hammer is missing and turns to Loki for help. Suspecting that a Jötunn has stolen it, Loki borrows the marvellous plumage of Freya and flies to Jötunheim to find out what has happened. Once in Jötunheim he soon discovers that Trym, the king of the frost-giants, has taken the hammer and hidden it twenty-four leagues underground.

[64] Jung, *CW* 10 § 57.
[65] Jung, *CW* 9, i § 117.

Anxious that with their newly acquired might the Jötunns will storm Asgard, the Æsir devise a plan to get the hammer back. The ransom that Trym has asked for—Freya's hand in marriage—is out of the question; people will say that the goddess is man-crazy if she goes to Jötunheim! But Trym's request gives Heimdall an idea. They will trick the Jötunns by disguising Thor as Freya! That will get him into Jötunheim and near enough to the hammer to turn the tables on the Jötunns.

Dressed as a bride, with Loki as his bridesmaid, Thor sets off to retrieve Mjöllnir. When the bridegroom Trym first sets eyes on his intended, he is taken aback by the sight of her. The goddess's appetite astonishes him. Upon arriving in Jötunheim the bride-to-be immediately consumes an ox, eight salmon, and three barrels of mead, not to mention other delicacies, which she also devours in great quantity. Reassuring the incredulous Trym, Loki informs him that Freya hadn't eaten for eight days, such had been her desire to come to him. Looking into Thor's rage-filled eyes, taking them to be Freya's, Trym is troubled by their fiery brightness. But again Loki reassures him that this is only because Freya has not slept for eight nights, so great is her longing to be his bride. These explanations are enough to assuage the Jötunn's doubts and the wedding service begins. As it is the custom in those Northern climes to solemnize weddings by placing Thor's hammer in the lap of the bride, Thor has only to await his moment. Everything goes off according to Heimdall's plan. Trym produces the hammer and places it on his bride's lap. Quickly seizing the hammer by its handle, the berserk Thor bursts from his disguise, slaying Trym and all his stock with immediate dispatch.

Enacting itself in Jung's thought, the lost hammer of Thor corresponds to Jung's account of our contemporary unconsciousness with respect to the reality of the psyche, the giants who stole his hammer to the rationalism and materialism of the nineteenth and twentieth centuries. While in previous centuries Thor had had a relatively firm grip on his hammer insofar as there then existed "a religious formula for everything psychic,"[66] the consciousness to which we were awakened with the Enlightenment rendered us more or less unconscious of the psychic factor and its power. Like Thor's Mjöllnir, buried twenty-four leagues beneath the earth in Jötunheim, the spiritual force or psychic factor was projected into the mysteries of matter and the forces of the natural world with the result that the sense of its agency and autonomy was quickly lost to the

---

[66] Jung, CW 9i § 11.

materialism of the science that had in this way come to the fore. Doubtless, this kind of projection, whatever forms it takes, has always been ubiquitous. The forces of the outside world frequently are immense enough to steal the psyche's reaction even as they seem to be the source of everything. The traumatized war veteran knows only too well what it is like to be pummelled night after night by intolerable scenes of battle. However, inasmuch as the myths (and eventually the recurring battle nightmares as well) are not merely copies of external objects and outer events, but, at the same time, impactful fantasies expressive of the psyche's own nature, the hammer is also retrieved. Knowing this we may imagine the theft of Thor's hammer and his subsequent reclaiming of it to be archetypal dimensions of any myth or image. For, while the external world does have an immense impact on the imagination, the fact that this impact is registered asymmetrically by such fantastic figures as frost-giants and boulder-demons points to the creative impact of a pre-existing inner world.[67] *A priori* this world, too, is a shaping spirit, as powerful in its own way as external objects and external causes.[68] And though Freud would

---

[67] In describing the psyche's response as "asymmetrical" I wish to capture in a single word Jung's view that images are not mere copies of the external world, but are also a function of the psyche's own objective character. Jung describes the asymmetrical quality of the psyche in a 1934 letter. While reading from this letter we may let his use of the image of an empty sack remind us of the image from our Northern myth in which Thor struggles in vain to open the sack of provisions which Útgarða-Loki has tied shut with the magic yarn of illusion. In this way we will appreciate once again how Thor enacts himself in Jung's thought: "The unconscious is on no account an empty sack in which the refuse of consciousness is collected, as it appears to be in Freud's view; it is the whole other half of the living psyche. More than that, it is a psychic reflection of the whole world. If you go into these problems you will soon see that our ego is situated between two antithetical worlds—the so-called outer world open to the senses, and the unconscious psychic substrate which alone enables us to grasp the world at all. This psychic substrate must necessarily be different from [i.e., asymmetrical—G. M.] the so-called outer world, otherwise there would be no possibility of grasping it, for like cannot cognize like" (Jung, *Letters*, vol. I, p. 143).

[68] It might be asked how Jung's claim to be a scientist can be squared with his having posited an unknown psychic factor which he frequently equates with spirit. Helpful in this regard is an article by the Canadian philosopher, logician and mathematician William Hatcher, "A Scientific Proof of the Existence of God" (*Journal of Baha'i Studies*, December 1993 - March 1994, pp. 1-16). In this article Hatcher argues that just as we are obliged to infer the existence of gravity from the fact that a falling object always moves downward towards the earth against the probability of randomness, so we are also obliged to infer the existence of a force to account for the fact that evolution has fostered increasingly complex systems against the probability of disorder and hazard. This force which produces evolution and which Hatcher further argues may be rationally called God, I believe, may be likened to, or even identified with, that *a priori* psychic factor which in Jung's view produces both archetypal phenomena and that further expression of evolution, individuation.

derive this inner world from the world of external objects through a process called introjection, which he conceived to be as voluminous in its capacity to swallow up and take in as were the ravenous Loki and the barrel-chested Thor, Jung recognized that what would seem to have been introjected from the external world is always already amalgamated with fantasies which the psyche has extruded via the process of projection. Like the four-year-old child who eats his broccoli only when his story-telling mother tells him it is a wonderful green tree, what is taken into the psyche through introjection is complicated from the start by the giants of imagination with which it must compete. Again, it is impossible due to the lack of an Archimedean position to say which strikes first, the inner world or the outer, or which process is more primary, introjection or projection. Our myth, however, does not trouble itself with this chicken-or-egg dilemma regarding priority in the process. Rather, it dramatizes the relationship of these powers and principalities through tales which are indicative of the way things happen. Jung, arguing for the non-derivative reality of the psychic factor, lives out these patterns again for our times and for our discipline, as does Freud in arguing the contrary case.[69]

Passages from Jung's writings in which we witness Jung reclaiming for psychology the conceptual equivalent of the lost hammer of Thor are many. Before examining a few of these, let us note that, as with Thor, Jung also had to clothe himself in feminine attire before descending into the Jötunheim of his own unconscious in search of the psyche's objective

---

[69] In Freud's view, those psychic structures which Jung takes to be transparent to a psychic factor *sui generis* can in fact be accounted for in a manner consistent with his program of rigorous materialism. What Jung sees as archetypal structures with constructive-synthetic possibilities, Freud identified as the super-ego, particularly in its aspect as ego-ideal. The id, unwilling to relinquish a satisfaction, attempts to regain what it has in fact lost in the course of its clash with the external world, on the level of the ego-ideal. "Whereas the ego is essentially the representative of the external world, of reality, the super-ego stands in contrast to it as the representative of the internal world, of the id. Conflicts between the ego and the ideal will, as we are now prepared to find, ultimately reflect the contrast between what is real and what is psychical, between the external world and the internal world" (*The Ego and the Id*, p. 26). Reading this psycho-physics phylogenetically, as was Freud's tendency, we get a dialectical materialist account of what Jung, with reference to spirit, called archetypes: "Through the forming of the ideal, what biology and the vicissitudes of the human species have created in the id and left behind in it is taken over by the ego and re-experienced in relation to itself as an individual. Owning to the way in which the ego ideal is formed, it has the most abundant links with the phylogenetic acquisitions of each individual— his archaic heritage" (p. 26). Without abandoning his materialistic standpoint, Freud, too, has a story of how Thor's hammer is retrieved. We shall return to these ideas in the third chapter, insighting them there through the myth of Baldr's death.

reality. And like Thor, Jung was initially loath to don such garb. Commenting on this in his 1925 seminar on analytical psychology, Jung reports that at the outset of his career autonomous fantasy thinking was utterly repugnant to him. "Permitting fantasy in myself had the same effect on me as would be produced on a man if he came into his workshop and found all the tools flying about doing things independently of his will. It shocked me … to think of the possibility of a fantasy life in my own mind; it was against the intellectual ideals I had developed for myself."[70] To defend himself from the shocking recognition that the workshop tools of his mind frequently did get out of his conscious grip (even as Thor's hammer got out of his), Jung, as he put it, projected his material onto Miss Miller, the subject whose fantasies he explored in the pages of his *Wandlungen*.[71] Only later, with his recognition of the anima as an inner figure in himself, was he able to embrace this autonomous fantasy thinking as springing from the depths of his own nature. It was the otherness of this apparently subjective factor that intimated to Jung the existence of an objective psyche. He could no more have grasped the reality of this factor without his encounter with the anima than could Thor have regained Mjöllnir without donning the wedding dress of Freya.

As early as 1912, in the series of lectures which he gave at Fordham University in New York titled "The Theory of Psychoanalysis," we can already witness Jung reaching for, but not yet quite retrieving, Thor's hammer.

> We must never forget that the world is, in the first place, a subjective phenomenon. *The impressions we receive from these accidental happenings are also our own doing.* It is not true that the impressions are forced on us unconditionally; our own predisposition conditions the impression. A man whose libido is blocked will have, as a rule, quite different and very much more vivid impressions than one whose libido is organized in a wealth of activities. A person who is sensitive in one way or another will receive a deep impression from an event which would leave a less sensitive person cold.[72]

---

[70] Jung, *Analytical Psychology*, pp. 27-28.
[71] Jung, *Analytical Psychology: Notes of the Seminar given in 1925*, pp. 27-28.
[72] Jung, *CW* 4 § 400.

The context of this quotation is a critique of the trauma theory in the aetiology of hysteria. Though Jung, doubtless, is drawing heavily on Freud's view that "there is no 'indication of reality' in the unconscious, so that one cannot distinguish between truth and fiction that has been cathected with affect,"[73] the concept of "innate sensitiveness,"[74] which Jung introduces a paragraph earlier in his text, is an early conceptualization of the innate psychic factor, which he will later describe, toward the latter part of his career, as the objective psyche and the philosopher's stone. From our vantage point, however, this factor is Mjöllnir, the hammer of Thor, flashing in the distance like the lightning of that god.

Another quotation, from a passage published just two years later, is far bolder in its claim, for here the context is a discussion of the "tendencies or determinants which produce culture in man with the same logic as in the bird they produce the artfully woven nest, and antlers in the stag":

> The purely causal, not to say materialistic views of the last few decades seek to explain all organic formation as the reaction of living matter, and though this is undoubtedly a heuristically valuable line of inquiry, as far as any real explanation goes it amounts only to a more or less ingenious postponement and apparent minimizing of the problem. ... External causes can account for at most half the reaction, the other half is due to the peculiar attributes of living matter itself, without which the specific reaction formation could never come about at all. We have to apply this principle also in psychology. The psyche does not merely *react*, it gives its own specific answer to the influences at work upon it, and at least half the resulting formation is entirely due to the psyche and the determinants inherent within it.[75]

Though Jung had not yet hit upon the concept of the archetype, and though only with the development of that concept did he take Mjöllnir fully in hand, there is already a Mjöllnir-like quality to his assertion that "[t]he psyche does not merely *react*, [but] it gives its own answer to the influences at work upon it." The images through which the psyche responds to the influences at work upon it, be they images

---

[73] Sigmund Freud, *The Origins of Psychoanalysis: Letters to Wilhelm Fliess, Drafts and Notes: 1892-1899*, tr. E. Mosbacher & J. Strachey (New York: Basic Books, 1954), L: September 21, 1897, p. 264.
[74] Jung, *CW* 4 § 399.
[75] Jung, *CW* 4 § 665.

such as we find in collective myths or images such as those we find in our own dreams and fantasies, are as the lightning hurled by Thor. While we are daily pelted from without by a barrage of stimuli, some of which may be of a traumatic intensity, there is a psychic factor which at the same time strikes outward from within. In this connection, a few lines of a patient's poem come to mind:

> I write in the hope that the world will disappear,
> Continually frustrated by its refusal to do so.
> Occasionally I succeed.
> The world retreats a little,
> Just enough to allow a poem.[76]

Earlier in this chapter we asked how it is that the psyche is so constituted that when we are stuck or bogged down it generates images of such vitality, sagacity, and compelling power that we are enabled to change direction or move ahead again. Continuing our exploration, let us now examine two quotations from Jung's writings in which he not only regains Thor's hammer, but brings it resoundingly to bear upon this question. In the first quotation, Jung merely reiterates his views regarding the compensatory tendency of the unconscious, accounting for these through the archetypes. In the second quotation, he gives a more explanatory account. This is the first:

> Every invasion of the unconscious is an answer to a definite conscious situation, and this answer follows from the totality of possible ideas present, i.e., from the total disposition which ... is a simultaneous picture *in potentia* of psychic existence. The splitting up into single units, its one-sided and fragmentary character, is of the essence of consciousness. The reaction coming from the disposition always has a total character, as it reflects a nature which has not been divided up by any discriminating consciousness. Hence its overpowering effect. It is the unexpected, all-embracing, completely illuminating answer, which works all the more as illumination and revelation since the conscious mind has got itself wedged into a hopeless blind alley.[77]

---

[76] In other stanzas of this poem (or in other sessions of its author's therapy), we may imagine the opposite movement: the poem receding a little, just enough to allow the world.

[77] Jung, *CW* 11 § 900.

The more explanatory account comes from Jung's 1925 seminar. With Thor's hammer in mind, let us take note of Jung's use of the word "repercussions." Though he uses it but once in the section quoted here, it actually appears three times in the paragraph from which this is excerpted. In a similar vein, that is to say, with the image of Mjöllnir buried twenty-four leagues beneath the earth in Jötunheim in mind, let us also take note of Jung's reference to the archetype being "dug up" through analytical work from the external world in which it is buried by unconscious projections.

> ... [T]he images of the collective unconscious ... [while] refer[ring] to the influences of absolutely existing external objects ... are the psychic reactions to them, the only difference between the image of external reality and the archetype being that the former is conscious and the latter unconscious. The archetype nonetheless appears also in the so-called external world if it is not "dug up" in ourselves by an analytical procedure. But you can apply the same analytical processes to the image of external reality also, and see how subjective they are. ... archetypes are records of reactions to subjective sense-images. In our conscious memory we record things as they are subjectively, as memories of real facts, but in the unconscious we record the subjective reactions to the facts as we perceive them in the conscious. I should suppose that there are layers even of such repercussions, reactions of reactions, and that they would form the stratification of the mind.[78]

In the next paragraph, Jung gives an example of this process, and in the paragraph after that he makes the decisive swerve which our myth describes as the regaining of Mjöllnir by Thor. We now quote an excerpt from the former paragraph together with the whole of the later one.

> ... [T]he most regular recurrence in the world is the rising and the setting of the sun. Our consciousness remembers the real facts of this phenomenon, but our unconscious has recorded the untold millions of sunrises and sunsets in the form of a hero myth, and the hero myth is the expression of the way in which our unconscious has reacted to the conscious image of sunrise and sunset. As reaction *a* is

---

[78] Jung, *Analytical Psychology*, p. 135.

forming the image of the external world, so reaction *b* is forming the collective unconscious—what one could call a sort of mirage world or reflex world.

But it would be somewhat of a depreciation to make the dignity of the collective unconscious one of secondhand origin only. ... [A consideration of another kind] allows us to envisage the collective unconscious as a firsthand phenomenon, something *sui generis*.... As we assume that behind our image of the external world there is an absolute entity, so necessarily we must assume that behind the perceiving subject there is an entity; and when we start our consideration from that end, we must say the collective unconscious is reaction *a*, or the first reaction, or first image of the world, while the conscious would be second hand only.[79]

Jung's reference to the collective unconscious as "a sort of mirage world or reflex world," along with the possibility he raises of its being a "firsthand phenomenon," are redolent of our Northern myths. We have only to think of the reflexive feats performed by Thor in the mirage world of Útgarða-Loki's castle, or, again, of Thor's having disguised himself up as Freya in order to retrieve his hammer from Jötunheim, to glimpse the Northern lights emanating from these passages.

Thor, Jung, and the Jötunn Rungne

To complete our encounter with the aspect of the psyche which we have been amplifying throughout this chapter by comparing the stories of Thor with the resembling theories of psychoanalysis and analytical psychology, let us examine one last juxtaposition of images and theories, if only to gain another glimpse of the Northern light that has inspired these pages.

In his essay, "A Study in the Process of Individuation," Jung presents the case study of an American woman of Scandinavian descent who, immediately prior to her sessions with Jung, had visited Denmark, her mother's country.[80] The series of mandala paintings that she produced in the course of her analysis began with a dark, brooding, Northern landscape of craggy rocks and sea. The second picture of the series, which

---

[79] Jung, *Analytical Psychology*, p. 136.
[80] Jung, *CW* 9i § 525.

is the one that I want to single out here, is of lightning striking the rocky shoreline and blasting out from the mass of stone a round, illuminated boulder. This boulder becomes elaborated in subsequent paintings into

Thor clothed as Freya speeding to Jötunheim to retrieve his hammer, his chariot wheels rimmed with lightning

a number of complicated mandalas. This development, Jung argues, compensates the turmoil of his patient's outer life insofar as it reflects an inner process of self-realization or individuation. Surprisingly, Jung, in his extensive amplification of this picture, neglects to mention Thor, whose chariot wheels rimmed with lightning are continuous with the mandala symbolism he explores. As I now, through this mere mention, bring that boulder-smashing Northern god of the lightning flash into relation with this patient's painting, I am reminded not to neglect another of his stories. Told in its archaic, Northern version, it is the tale of Thor's fight with the Jötunn Rungne. As enacted in Jung's thought, it is the tale of the interpenetrating oneness of matter and spirit which is one aspect of alchemy's philosopher's stone.

I will not recount the Norse tale in its entirety, but only the part that bears on our theme.

When summoned to the aid of the other Æsir deities who had gotten themselves in a conflict with Rungne, the largest of the Jötunns, Thor immediately faced him in battle. Arguing that it would be no victory for Thor to defeat an unarmed Jötunn, Rungne persuaded Thor to allow him to fetch his weapons—a shield and whetstone—from Jötunheim. Fearing that these weapons would not be sufficient, Rungne's Jötunn backers created a battle-mate for him out of clay and a mare's heart. As immense as this creature was, however, it was gutless compared to Rungne himself, whose heart was a triangular stone. When they met in battle, Thor stormed Rungne from all sides, like the lightning in Jung's patient's painting surrounding the boulder which it blasts from the shoreline. When Rungne threw his whetstone at Thor (again think of the boulder blasted free in the patient's painting), Thor hurled his hammer and smashed the stone in mid-air. Some of the shards fell on the ground, becoming the source of the whetstones used by our ancestors; others flew into Thor's head. Though Thor ultimately prevailed over his Jötunn foe, the whetstones that had lodged in his head embedded themselves there so deeply that they could never be removed.

Jung, in the context of his alchemical studies, tells a similar tale of a "stone" embedded in us from which our lives become. Let us conclude this chapter with his version:

> Something of the projection-carrier always clings to the projection, and even if we succeed to some degree in

integrating into our consciousness the part we recognize as psychic, we shall integrate along with it something of the cosmos and its materiality; or rather, since the cosmos is infinitely greater than we are, we shall have been assimilated by the inorganic. "Transform yourselves into living philosophical stones!" cries an alchemist, but he did not know how infinitely slowly the stone "becomes." ... In these projections we encounter the phenomenology of an "objective" spirit, a true matrix of psychic experience, the most appropriate symbol for which is matter. Nowhere and never has man controlled matter without closely observing its behaviour and paying heed to its laws, and only to the extent that he did so could he control it. The same is true of that objective spirit which today we call the unconscious: it is refractory like matter, mysterious and elusive, and obeys laws which are so non-human or suprahuman that they seem to us like a *crimen laesae majestatis humanae*. If a man puts his hand to the opus, he repeats, as the alchemists say, God's work of creation. The struggle with the unformed, with the chaos of Tiamat, is in truth a primordial experience.[81]

---

[81] Jung, *CW* 13 § 286.

CHAPTER TWO

Barnstock and the Volsungs: The Sword of Incest and the Tree of Life in Freud, Jung, and Spielrein

Yggdrasill, the Rainbow Bridge, and the Æsir

Every time two families become connected by a marriage, each of them thinks itself superior to or of better birth than the other. Of two neighbouring towns each is the other's most jealous rival …. Closely related races keep one another at arm's length; the South German cannot endure the North German, the Englishman casts every kind of aspersion upon the Scot …. [G]reater differences … lead to an almost insuperable repugnance, such as the Gallic people feel for the German, the Aryan for the Semite ….

—Sigmund Freud, *Group Psychology and the Analysis of the Ego*, pp. 130-131

… [T]he tree symbolizes life. It is alive like a human being, with head, feet, etc., and it lives longer than man, so it is impressive, there is mana in a tree. … Formerly a tree was planted when a child was born, and as long as the tree lived the child lived. … Trees through their fruits are nourishing, so they acquire a mother quality. There is a Germanic legend that the ash and the alder were the first two human beings. … Then there is the world-tree, Yggdrasill, with its roots in the earth and its branches in Heaven; the first life came from that tree, and at the end of the world the last couple will be buried in Yggdrasill; human life begins and ends in the tree.

—C. G. Jung, *Dream Analysis: Notes of the Seminar Given in 1929-1930*, pp. 360-361

Runic Preamble

J ung begins his essay, "The Philosophical Tree," by quoting a brief passage from Goethe's *Faust*: "All theory, my friend, is grey, /But green life's golden tree."[1] In this chapter, we shall again be dealing with theories—the theories of Freud and Jung. In keeping with the lines of verse Jung quotes from *Faust*, we shall also be dealing with a tree. To actual trees, such as those studied by Gustave Senn, the professor of botany for whose *Festschrift* Jung wrote his seminal essay, the tree that will concern us in these pages stands in something of the same relationship as does Mjöllnir, the hammer of Thor, to lightning, or the hero myth to the endlessly repeating cycle of the rising and setting sun. While being like these mythic images in that it too is related asymmetrically to the natural phenomenon upon which it is partially modelled, this tree-as-image (or better, image-as-tree) reflects the fact that the hammer-wielding, lightning-hurling psyche has also the character of a natural growth process. This is so, it is important to add, even with respect to images that are not explicitly tree-like. Just as the archetype, according to archetypal psychology, "is wholly immanent to its image,"[2] so that aspect of the psyche which mythologizes itself in terms of a tree is an archetypal potential of any event, any image. In this connection, we may think of the symbolic stone of the alchemists, which was at the same time not a stone, but a thousand other things besides.[3] In an equally philosophical sense, the tree by means of which we shall be imagining in these pages is not a tree only, but the house of a family and the sword of a hero as well.

At the centre of the North-European mythological cosmos stands the World Ash, Yggdrasill, the most famous tree of Norse mythology. Nine worlds are housed in the roots and branches of this great tree: Asgard (the home of the Æsir), Jötunheim (the home of the giants), Midgard (the middle earth of human habitation), Hel (the underworld realm of the dead), Ljossalheim (the realm of light, elves and air-spirits), Vanaheim (the realm of land and sea-deities), Svartalfheim (the realm of black elves, stone spirits, and dwarves), Niflheim (the realm of ice and cold) and Muspellheim (the realm of fire and heat). Lesser known is Barnstock, the ancient oak that shelters the ancestral home of the

---

[1] C. G. Jung, *Collected Works*, tr. R. F. C. Hull (Princeton, NJ: Princeton University Press, 1953), vol. 13, para. 252. All subsequent references to Jung's *Collected Works (CW)*, vols. 1-20, will be by volume and paragraph number (designated by §), except in the case of text from prefaces and tables which will be by volume and page number.

[2] James Hillman, "On the Necessity of Abnormal Psychology: Ananke and Athene," in J. Hillman, ed. *Facing the Gods* (Irving, TX.: Spring Publications, 1980), p. 10.

[3] Jung, *CW* 9i § 555; *CW* 11 § 707; *CW* 13 § 381n.9; *CW* 14 § 626, 643.

Volsungs, the line from which Sigmund and Sigurd (Siegfried) trace their descent. Like Yggdrasill, this tree is as laden with fantasies as the trees of nature are with branches and leaves. And just as the botanist learns much about his science from actual leaves and branches, so we learn much about the psyche from Barnstock's imaginal leaves and mythical branches. The corollary of this is also true, as Jung's quote from Goethe implies: our theories of the psyche, though seemingly defoliate and grey, are themselves expressions of "life's green and golden tree."[4]

An enormous oak, Barnstock (Barnstokkr = child-trunk) is the *axis familias* around which the home of the Volsungs is built, even as Yggdrasill, the cosmic tree which houses the nine worlds, is the *axis mundi*. Beneath the sheltering canopy of its branches live Volsung, the king of the Huns, his ten sons, and a daughter. Foremost among the sons is the eldest, Sigmund, who, in his turn, becomes father of the renowned dragon-slaying hero Sigurd. Signy, the twin sister of Sigmund, who is given in marriage to the wicked Goth Siggeur as part of an ill-fated attempt to forge a peace alliance between the two clans, becomes mother, in her turn, of a son, Sinfjotli, through an incestuous union with her brother. Born of incest, Sinfjotli is of pure Volsung blood. Faithful to the vengeful ambitions that led his mother to conceive him, and heeding the impulses of his doubly Volsung bloodline, Sinfjotli, along with his father/uncle Sigmund, slays Siggeur and his kin in retribution for Siggeur's treacherous killing of Volsung and nine of the ten Volsung sons shortly after his marriage to Signy.

---

[4] Here we might ask what imaginal trees might have to tell us about actual trees. Jung, after all, wrote his paper on the philosophical tree to honour a professor of botany. We do well to address this point lest we give the mistaken impression that we regard the tree that shall concern us in this chapter semiotically, as a metaphor of merely hermeneutic significance, when in fact it is a veritable tree of life. In taking as its empirical starting point what sciences such as contemporary botany discard as error (the better to interrogate the projections psyche makes), analytical psychology embraces and affirms an asymmetrical relationship to the other sciences. While those sciences, as highly differentiated extensions of the perceptual organs, classify and describe the features and properties of the extrapsychic phenomena that have long been the contents of our conscious experience (for instance, actual trees such as the Northern ash and oak), depth psychology, in Jung's sense, clarifies and describes the psyche's subjective reaction to those same, less objectively perceived, phenomena (imaginal trees such as Yggdrasill and Barnstock). In doing so, paradoxically enough, psychology isolates within the retort of its own particular methodological process a spirit of life which the other life sciences seek in vain in the physiological process that they take to be their object— hence the relevance of Jung's "Philosophical Tree" to a botanist's *Festschrift*.

Barnstock in the Thought of Freud and Jung

> It has justly been said that the Oedipus complex is the
> nuclear complex of the neuroses .... It represents the peak
> of infantile sexuality, which, through its after-effects,
> exercises a decisive influence on the sexuality of adults. ...
> With the progress of psychoanalytic studies the importance
> of the Oedipus complex has become more and more evident;
> its recognition has become the shibboleth that distinguishes
> the adherents of psychoanalysis from its opponents.[5]
>
> —Sigmund Freud

> *Participation mystique* obtains between parents and children.
> ... So long as *participation mystique* with the parents persists,
> a relatively infantile style of life can be maintained. Through
> the *participation mystique* life is pumped into us from outside
> in the form of unconscious motivations, for which, since
> they are unconscious, no responsibility is felt. Because of this
> infantile unconsciousness the burden of life is lightened. ...
> One is not alone, but exists unconsciously in twos or threes.
> In imagination the son is in his mother's lap, protected by
> the father. The father is reborn in the son—at least as a link
> in the chain of eternal life.[6]
>
> —C. G. Jung

Listening to the sagas of his patient's lives, Freud was well aware of
the passions and treacheries, incestuous impulses and murderous
fantasies that are rife beneath the surface of family life. Borrowing a name
from Greek mythology, he placed these family imbroglios under the rubric
of the Oedipus complex even as our Northern saga places them beneath
the branches of Barnstock. Had Freud spoken of a Barnstock complex
rather than an Oedipus complex, however, he might have understood
better the saga that was brewing in the branches of his own psychoanalytic
tree. For, while Freud was refining his theories about the role of the
Oedipal drama in hysteria and obsessional neurosis, his Teutonic heir
apparent, Jung, was listening to his first analytic patient, the young

---

[5] Sigmund Freud, *Three Essays on Sexuality,* in *The Freud Pelican Library,* vol. 7, p.
149-150n.
[6] Jung, *CW* 10 § 70.

Russian woman Sabina Spielrein, as she discussed her fantasies of Siegfried, the incestuous love-child that had been conceived in her psyche through her transference to Jung.

Conceived like Sinfjotli, the son by incest of Signy and Sigmund, the Siegfried fantasy of Spielrein and Jung was latent with a very different conception of psychoanalysis from the one Freud had in mind when he installed Jung as the president of the International Psychoanalytic Association. Indeed, like Sinfjotli of the Volsunga Saga, Jung's vision of the psyche, grounded as it was in a very different understanding of the interpretation of myth, was destined to destroy an alliance—in this case the one Freud had sought to establish between Vienna and the scientifically prestigious Zürich School. For though Jung, highly esteeming Freud, characterized his relation to the older man as that of a son to a respected father,[7] and though Freud, following suit, compared their relationship to that between Moses and Joshua,[8] Jung was no more Freud's son than was Sinfjotli of the doubly-Hun blood the son of the Goth Siggeur.

Reputed to be the great-grandson of Goethe,[9] Jung was acutely aware of the Germanic blood flowing in his veins. Linked to this illustrious forebear through his experience of that older soul in himself which he had, early in life, learned to call "personality No. 2,"[10] Jung could never restrict his vision of the psyche to the family romance to which "personality No. 1," the ordinary child and adolescent, was subject. Straining against what he experienced as the swaddling bands of Freud's personalistic psycho-sexual theories,[11] Jung immersed himself in mythological research, a sphere of enquiry more congruent with his experience of personality No. 2. Of course, as Freud was only too aware, the mythical Oedipus had made a similar move: he, too, had tried to

---

[7] William McGuire, ed. *The Freud/Jung Letters: The Correspondence between Sigmund Freud and C. G. Jung*, tr. R. Manheim & R. F. C. Hull (Princeton, N.J.: Princeton University Press, 1974), p. 122.

[8] McGuire, ed. *The Freud/Jung Letters*, pp. 196-197. Freud wrote to Jung, "... [I]f I am Moses, then you are Joshua and will take possession of the promised land of psychiatry, which I shall only be able to glimpse from afar."

[9] C. G. Jung, *Memories, Dreams, Reflections*, ed. A. Jaffé (New York: Random House, 1965), p. 35.

[10] Jung, *Memories, Dreams, Reflections*, pp. 45-48, 66, 74, 75, 80.

[11] Jung would express this attitude much later in his Tavistock Lectures: "... I often scratch my head at a meeting and say, 'Are they all midwifes and nurses?' Does not the world consist chiefly of parents and grandparents? The adults have the problems. Leave the poor children alone. I get the mother by the ears and not the child. The parents make the neuroses of children." Jung, *CW* 18 § 296.

evade the fate of incest and parricide in one home only to run afoul of it in another. Hoping that Jung would ultimately give up his incestuous claims upon the psychoanalytic domain and transform his rivalrous feelings into affectionate ones, Freud viewed Jung's spirited innovations and revisionist accounts at first with the tolerance of a father who knows better and then with an increasingly jaundiced eye.

For a more coherent understanding of the heresy that flowed in Jung's veins,[12] Freud might better have looked to our Northern saga for perspective. Viewed from this vantage point, Jung was less like Oedipus leaving the home of foster-parents whom he erroneously believed to be his real parents, and more like Sinfjotli turning against his stepfather Siggeur, loyal to the promptings of his doubly-Volsung blood. Simply put, the issue was this: if the sonship bestowed upon him by Freud meant being bound by Freud's signature terms, infantile sexuality and Oedipus complex, Jung would have to reject this sonship and rise up against the Siggeur whom he met in Freud by endogamously conceiving, on the model of Sigmund and Signy, versions of these notions that better suited his age-old Volsung soul. And so it was, ironically enough—through such Jungian terms as *participation mystique*, parental imago, introversion, the racial unconscious, endogamous kinship libido, and symbolic (not literal) incest—that the asymmetrical psychic factor, which mythologizes itself in terms of pure blood lines, ethnic roots, and the "insuperable repugnance" of one clan for another, came to enact itself again in the very concepts in which it was being theorized about.

Far from trying to avoid his mythic fate in the manner of Oedipus, Jung endeavoured to embrace it as his destiny, turning the passive incestuous and parricidal wishes that are so characteristic of the neurotic (according to Freud's views) into the rejuvenating active incest and emancipating act of sacrifice by which the ego, modelling itself on the consciousness-creating redemptive hero, both renews itself in and frees itself from its matrix in the unconscious.

In a late preface to *Symbols of Transformation*, the extensively revised and "much pruned" version of *Wandlungen und Symbole der Libido* (the book which "cost [him] Freud's friendship"[13]), Jung writes:

---

[12] Here I allude to the following statement from Jung's March 3, 1912 letter to Freud: "I would never have sided with you in the first place had not heresy run in my blood." McGuire, ed. *The Freud/Jung Letters*, p. 491.

[13] Jung, *Memories, Dreams, Reflections*, p. 167.

The psyche is not of today; its ancestry goes back many millions of years. Individual consciousness is only the flower and the fruit of a season, sprung from the perennial rhizome beneath the earth; and it would find itself in better accord with the truth if it took the existence of the rhizome into its calculations. For the root matter is the mother of all things.[14]

What Jung so confidently affirms about the psyche's ancestral roots in this late preface was rife with conflict for him at the beginning of his psychoanalytic career, Freud's influence having constellated in him a countering or compensatory introversion of libido. Indeed, as Jung goes on to say in this preface with respect to himself at that time: "... I simply had to know what unconscious or preconscious myth was forming me, from what rhizome I sprang."[15] In this regard, Jung, despite the sonship he at that time still felt toward Freud, was not unlike the mythical hero he described in *Wandlungen* who becomes his own father and gives birth to himself.[16]

In adopting Jung as his son and heir, Freud, like the Siggeur of our Northern saga, failed to recognize the archetypal fantasies latent in the disparate bloodlines he hoped to intermingle in order to prevent psychoanalysis from becoming a ghettoized affair, of concern only to Jews.[17] Blood being thicker than water, however, the mix he sought to bring about could not be made, at least not at that time and with that end in mind. Motivated less by an antipathy such as Freud's for the Jewishness of psychoanalysis than by a need to find support for his own ideas from within that sphere of the unconscious that his experience of personality No. 2 had intimated to him was the source of the authority that one bestows upon a father,[18] Jung, after the pattern of Sinfjotli, responded to being adopted as Freud's heir by acquainting himself with the ancestral rhizome from which his individual consciousness and personality No. 1—the flower and fruit of a season—ultimately sprang. Receiving the blood of his ancestors through this root or rhizome, Jung fortified himself against what he increasingly experienced as the watering down effects of Freud's theories of infantile sexuality. For his part, Freud

---

[14] Jung, *CW* 5, p. xxiv.
[15] Jung, *CW* 5, p. xxv.
[16] Jung, *CW* 5 § 332, 335, 497, 516.
[17] John Kerr, *A Most Dangerous Method: The Story of Jung, Freud, and Sabina Spielrein* (New York: Alfred A. Knopf, 1993), p. 287.
[18] Jung, *CW* 4 § 727.

found Jung's dilution of psychoanalytic doctrine even less palatable. As with the Huns and the Goths, the alliance between Vienna and Zürich, Freud and Jung, collapsed into a bitter, if not bloody, conflict.

Signy's Wedding

> At the time our poetry began, [Dr. Jung] had two girls, and the potentiality of a boy within him, which my unconscious ferreted out at the appropriate time in "prophetic dreams." He told me that he loved Jewish women, that he wanted to love a dark Jewish girl. So in him, too, the urge to remain faithful to his religion and culture, as well as the drive to explore other possibilities through a new race, the drive to liberate himself from the paternal edicts through an unbelieving Jewess. His friend is Prof. Freud—a Jew, old *pater familias*. I do not know whether it is reality or fantasy that Prof. Freud has six children. Here, too, the Christian is the "son" of the Jew. The latter is older and more independent. But at the same time my friend is my little son, so that *volens-nolens* we are married to Prof. Freud.[19]

—Sabina Spielrein, Diary entry for October 19, 1910

Enacting itself in Freud's thought as the theory of the Oedipus complex and in Jung's thought in the form of the rival concept of *participation mystique*, Barnstock, as we have already mentioned, is the mythical home of the Volsungs. An enormous oak tree, Barnstock's trunk rises up in the midst of a large hall in which Volsung resides with his daughter, Signy, and his ten sons, while its billowing branches stretch out through the roof. The roots of this tree are the family's ancestral lineage, the deepest root of which stretches back to the great Æsir deity and all-father, Óðinn. This divine progenitor invests the line of Volsung the Hun four times. In the first place, Óðinn is the father of Volsung's great-grandfather Sigi. In the second place, it is he who sends Rerir, the childless son of Sigi, the fertility apple through which his potency is restored and a son, Volsung, is born to him. In the third place, Óðinn's spirit again enters the lineage of this family through Volsung's marriage to Hljod, the wish-maiden who, at Óðinn's bidding, had brought Volsung's father Rerir the

---

[19] Cited in Aldo Carotenuto, *A Secret Symmetry: Sabina Spielrein Between Jung and Freud* (New York: Pantheon, 1982), p. 30.

aforementioned vitalizing apple which had enabled him to sire Volsung. The incestuous link to Óðinn then recurs a fourth time in the subsequent generation through the union between Volsung's eldest son, Sigmund, and his only daughter, Signy. Keeping in mind our earlier discussion of the different ways in which Barnstock enacts itself in the life and thought of Freud and Jung, let us now look more deeply at the dynamics of the incestuous impulse presented in the saga.

The Tale Retold

Signy, we are told, did not welcome marriage to the Goth king, Siggeur. Her father, Volsung, however, insisted on the union, for it was through unions such as these that Northern families forged the alliances that allowed their societies to survive in an age when there existed only a rudimentary collective judiciary and no effective central government.[20] *Though the reason for Signy's antipathy to the marriage is not stated in the saga, evidently it is figurative of the apprehension which was felt in the families of the ancient North about whether the alliances forged through marriage would provide the hoped-for defense against the larger social world, or whether, on the contrary, treachery would befall the family at the hands of its in-laws. Such treachery had already befallen Sigi, the son of Óðinn and grandfather of Volsung. His wife's brothers, whom he had taken into his trust, intrigued against him, killing him and his men in battle. His son, Rerir, lived to avenge his father, before siring, with the help of the apple sent by Óðinn, Signy's father, Volsung. It is little wonder, given this compensatory or dialectical pattern of treachery and incest, exogamy and endogamy, that Signy and her brother Sigmund, as well as their subsequent progeny, Sinfjotli and Sigurd, bear the root element of their great-great-(great) grandfather Sigi's name. This element, sig, in fact, goes back one more generation, to Óðinn himself, who was also known by the name, Sigtyr, the Victory God. The fact that the name of Signy's husband, Siggeur, also partakes of this name suggests that the same identity-preserving, incestuous pattern courses through his bloodline as well. It was actually a convention of many Scandinavian, Anglo-Saxon, and other Germanic royal families to trace their ancestral roots back to Óðinn. But as with the Goths and the Huns in the Volsunga Saga, these noble bloodlines did not mix any more easily on that account. Indeed, the contrary was often the case. For though literal blood is*

---

[20] Jesse Byock, *The Saga of the Volsungs: The Norse Epic of Sigurd the Dragon Slayer* (Berkeley & Los Angeles: University of California Press, 1990), p. 10.

thicker than water, metaphorical blood is thicker than both. Life as we live it is always a dilution of the archetypal imperative that compels and animates it—hence the strife to which marriage and family life are subject.

The wedding between Signy and Siggeur was held in the Hall of the Volsungs, beneath the branches of Barnstock. In ironic contradistinction to the phrase uttered by the priest or minister in contemporary Christian marriages—"What God has joined together, let no man put asunder"—the vows of the bride and groom of the saga were no sooner sworn before Óðinn than they were sundered by him. Appearing among the company of assembled families, Óðinn, in his traditional form of the one-eyed stranger, approached Barnstock bearing a magnificent sword called Gram. Raising the sword over his head, he then plunged it into the trunk of the tree to the hilt. "He who draws this sword out of the trunk shall receive it from me as a gift, and he himself shall prove that he has never carried a better sword than this one."[21] With this act, and these words, Óðinn, as we shall see, invested the line of the Volsungs yet another time.

One by one, the men from the two families, who had only moments ago solemnized an alliance with each other through a marriage, took up Óðinn's challenge and attempted to draw Gram from the trunk of Barnstock. Each time, however, the sword held fast. It was not until Sigmund took his turn that the sword came free. Óðinn had, evidently, fated him to be its bearer.

Enchanted by the fineness of Sigmund's sword, Siggeur offered to purchase it for triple its weight in gold. To this offer Sigmund replied, "You could have taken this sword from where it stood, no less than I did, if it were meant for you to carry it; but now that it has come first into my hands, you will never obtain it, even should you offer me all the gold you own."[22] Though he feigned indifference, Sigmund's scornful tone angered the envious Siggeur, who immediately turned to thoughts of treachery and revenge.

The next day, King Siggeur hastened to return to Gautland. Before leaving with her husband, Signy approached her father and pleaded with him not to send her away. "I do not wish to go away with Siggeur, nor do my thoughts laugh with him," she said to Volsung. "I know through my foresight and that special ability found in our family that if the marriage contract is not quickly dissolved, this union will bring us much misery."[23]

---

[21] Byock, *The Saga of the Volsungs*, p. 38.
[22] Byock, *The Saga of the Volsungs*, p. 39.
[23] Byock, *The Saga of the Volsungs*, p. 39.

The special ability found in the Volsung family to which Signy refers was called in the pagan North a Kynfylgja or "family fetch."[24] A fetch is a guardian spirit, the genius of an individual or family. Its existence, doubtless, was inferred from familial patterns affecting individual destiny such as those we have already discussed in connection with the ancestral roots of Barnstock. Contemporary psychological theory, of course, knows the fetch by other names.

Being a man of honour, Volsung could not accede to his daughter's request. Reproaching Signy for making such a petition to him, he reminded her of the shamefulness of breaking an agreement and of the ill-will that would thereby be stirred up between the newly allied families. Signy, he insisted, would go away with Siggeur as his wife.

It was only three months later that the calamity that Signy intuited would befall the Volsungs on account of her marriage to Siggeur came to pass. It had been planned that Volsung and his ten sons would visit the newly wedded couple in Gautland for a feast. The invitation that Siggeur had extended to his wife's father and brothers, however, was part of a devious plan on his part to punish Sigmund and wrest from him his sword. Assembling a large army, Siggeur waited in ambush for the arrival of his in-laws. In the ensuing battle, the Volsungs fought bravely, killing many of King Siggeur's men. Being altogether outnumbered, however, they could not finally prevail. Volsung was slain in the field and the ten brothers were taken prisoner. Signy, hoping to save her brothers, begged Siggeur not to kill them. Agreeing in part, Siggeur postponed their execution, leaving them manacled to a fallen tree trunk. From this predicament, Sigmund alone of the ten brothers survived. Years later, hoping to conceive a strong Volsung son who would avenge the deaths of her father and brothers, Signy, disguising herself as another woman, sought out her brother Sigmund and lay with him. Sinfjotli, the child of this union, after being initiated into the ways of heroic manhood by Sigmund, fulfilled this fated task alongside his father, slaying Siggeur and his entire clan.

The Sword of Incest in Freud, Jung, and Spielrein

All the changes that Jung has proposed to make in psychoanalysis flow from his intention to eliminate what is objectionable in the family-complexes, so as not to find it

---

[24] "*Kynfylgja* literally means family fetch. A fetch was a guardian spirit or supernatural attendant, usually female, associated with an individual or a family. The term is used here with the more abstract meaning of inherited characteristic or (bad) luck." Byock, *The Saga of the Volsungs*, p. 114.

again in religion and ethics. ... The Oedipus complex has a
merely "symbolic" meaning: the mother in it means the
unattainable, which must be renounced in the interests of
civilization; the father who is killed in the Oedipus myth is
the "inner" father, from whom one must set oneself free in
order to become independent. ... In this way a new religio-
ethical system has been created ... which was bound to re-
interpret, distort or jettison the factual findings of analysis.[25]

—Sigmund Freud

Earlier we drew an analogy between the alliance that Freud and Jung
sought to create between Vienna and Zürich and the alliance that
Volsung and Siggeur sought to create between their two families, the
Huns and the Goths, through Siggeur's marriage to Volsung's daughter
Signy. As in the Volsunga Saga, this alliance between theoretical schools
of psychology was not a stable one. Indeed, no sooner had filial
relations been established between Freud and Jung than resistances
developed between the two men. On the level of theory, the issue over
which their legendary parting of the ways arose was the interpretation
of the psychological significance of incest fantasies. Like Gram, the
sword which Óðinn had plunged into the trunk of Barnstock, the
incest question enacted its archetypal prerogative in the lives of Freud
and Jung by sundering the marriage they had sought to create between
their respective interests. Freud, as Jung put it in his memoirs, "clung
to the literal interpretation of [incest] and was unable to grasp the
spiritual significance of incest as a symbol."[26] For his part, Jung was
of the opinion that "incest signified a personal complication only in
the rarest cases."[27] In marked contrast to Freud, who maintained that
neurotics are disturbed by the actual incestuous desires and parricidal
wishes that they were first subject to as children and which are the
hallmarks of the Oedipus complex, Jung, after initially cleaving to this
view himself, gradually came to see in the same sort of material a
symbolic process of regression and transformation, rebirth and
renewal.[28] Far from being fixated in infantile sexuality as Freud

---

[25] Sigmund Freud, *On the History of the Psycho-Analytic Movement*, Standard
Edition, vol. 14, 62.
[26] Jung, *Memories, Dreams, Reflections*, p. 167.
[27] Jung, *Memories, Dreams, Reflections*, p. 167.
[28] Jung, *CW* 5 § 654-655.

maintained, the neurotic, Jung came to believe, only appears to be sequestered in the infantile history to which he had returned under the duress of an obstacle in his current life situation. It is on account of his reluctance to relinquish his former mode of adaptation that the neurotic finds himself unadapted in his present circumstances.[29] Prospectively considered, however, the regressive process was, for Jung, a necessary part of future adaptation inasmuch as it immersed the individual in the depths of his own being, rendering his subsequent adaptation more authentic and meaningful.[30]

The Signy of this psychoanalytic saga was Sabina Spielrein, the young Russian Jewess whom Jung undertook to treat as his first analytic patient, his "test case,"[31] as it were. Spielrein, who has the distinction within the psychoanalytic tradition of being the earliest patient to become a psychoanalyst, originally presented at the Burghölzli with symptoms of psychotic hysteria. As Jung makes clear in his account of her case in his essay, "The Freudian Theory of Hysteria," her psyche was particularly rife with the kind of fantasy material that Freud had used as the basis for his theories.[32] Jung's analysis of Spielrein, however, was not simply an opportunity for him to experiment with Freud's method and begin to differentiate something of his own viewpoint. As virtually the first case in the history of psychoanalysis to involve the concept of countertransference, Spielrein's analysis with Jung was as illustrative of Jung's unconscious resistances to the methods and interpretations he was applying to Spielrein under Freud's tutelage as it was of Spielrein's complexes and fantasies. Indeed, just as Signy complained to her father of her distaste for her intended husband

---

[29] Jung, *CW* 4 § 557-575.

[30] Jung, *CW* 5 § 351 writes: "The development of consciousness inevitably leads not only to separation from the mother, but to separation from the parents and the whole family circle and thus to a relative degree of detachment from the unconscious and the world of instinct. Yet the longing for this lost world continues and, when difficult adaptations are demanded, is forever tempting one to make evasions and retreats, to regress to the infantile past, which then starts throwing up the incestuous symbolism. If only this temptation were perfectly clear, it would be possible, with a great effort of will, to free oneself from it. But it is far from clear, because a new adaptation or orientation of vital importance can only be achieved in accordance with the instincts. Lacking this, nothing durable results, only a convulsively willed, artificial product which proves in the long run to be incapable of life. No man can change himself into anything from sheer reason; he can only change into what he potentially is."

[31] McGuire, ed. *The Freud/Jung Letters*, p. 228.

[32] Jung, *CW* 4 § 52-63.

Siggeur, so Spielrein complained about a loathing for her father. In the perverse defecation fantasies through which she symptomatically expressed her loathing,[33] Jung saw a symbol of his own distaste for Freud's vision of the psyche. In effect, what Jung, writing about the incestuous regression which attaches the patient temporarily to the analyst, later said about the prospective function of transference held true for him as well in his countertransference to Spielrein. Just as "the transference to the analyst builds a bridge across which the patient can get away from his family into reality," so the countertransference, in this case, provided Jung with a bridge that carried him beyond his sonship to Freud.[34] With Spielrein's cure, Jung's own cure—the cure of his anima from what he later described as the tyranny of Freud's influence—began.[35]

In the throes of the now much discussed transference-countertransference enactment with Sabina Spielrein that led him to transgress the boundaries of ethical conduct, Jung turned to Freud, in whom he found a benign counsellor. As he had done with Fliess in the case of Emma Eckstein, Freud took an indulgent view of Jung's behaviour toward his patient. So long as Jung was applying Freudian principles, the whole episode could be framed as the inevitable "laboratory explosion" that befalls any dedicated scientist.[36] When Spielrein turned to Freud about the whole affair, even as Signy in the Volsunga Saga turned to Volsung regarding Siggeur, Freud handled her petition adroitly, averting a scandal for Jung. It was not until he himself felt betrayed by Jung's re-interpretations of psychoanalytic doctrine that he found anything incestuous about Jung's claim to his psychoanalytic domain. In this regard, Freud's writing of *Totem and Taboo* may be seen as an enactment of Óðinn's plunging of the sword into Barnstock. Writing in counterpoint to the divergent views on mythology, incest, and the status of the infantile that Jung, his adopted son and Crown Prince, was simultaneously developing in *Wandlungen*, Freud sought to set out his own views on these matters.

---

[33] Jung, *CW* 4 § 55-56.

[34] Jung, *CW* 4 § 428.

[35] Expressed in the conceptual terms which Jung developed only much later, Spielrein was an earlier carrier of the anima figure that compensated the persona with which he, as President of the International Psychoanalytic Association, was identified. Cf. Jung, *CW* 7 § 304.

[36] McGuire, ed. *The Freud/Jung Letters*, p. 235.

Óðinn's Sword in Freud's Hands

It is not difficult to conceive of how Freud would have interpreted Óðinn's sword-brandishing appearance at the wedding feast beneath the branches of Barnstock. We have only to think of the similarity between this scene from our saga and the vision of the primordial family Freud provides in *Totem and Taboo*. Beneath the manifest content of the saga's story Freud would doubtless find a representation of what he, drawing on Darwin, called the "primal horde." Óðinn, in Freud's speculative reconstruction of human prehistory, would correspond to that jealous and dominating figure, the primal father, who held all the women, including his own daughters, in a horde over which he enjoyed exclusive sexual licence. The sword, the Volsung brothers, and their Goth brother-in-law Siggeur would correspond, likewise, to the castration threat by which the father drove the brothers out from the horde. At the same time, Freud would also see in these figures an archaic vestige of the so-called "primal crime," wherein the brothers banded together and slew their father.

Keeping in mind the scene from our saga in which the Volsung brothers, along with Siggeur and his contingent, compete to see which of them can draw the sword from Barnstock, let us quote the famous passage in which this scene enacts itself in Freud's thought:

> One day the brothers who had been driven out came together, killed and devoured their father and so made an end of the patriarchal horde. United, they had the courage to do and succeeded in doing what would have been impossible for them individually. ... The violent primal father had doubtless been the feared and envied model of each one of the company of brothers: and in the act of devouring him they accomplished their identification with him, and each one of them acquired a portion of his strength.[37]

Freud's vision of the aftermath of this prehistoric act of parricide is also resonant with our Northern saga, a variation of its theme:

> Though the brothers had banded together in order to overcome their father, they were all one another's rivals in

---

[37] Sigmund Freud, *Totem and Taboo: Some Points of Agreement between the Mental Lives of Savages and Neurotics*, tr. J. Strachey (New York: W. W. Norton, 1950), pp. 141-142.

regard to the women. Each of them would have wished, like his father, to have all the women to himself. The new organization would have collapsed in a struggle of all against all, for none of them was of such over-mastering strength as to be able to take on his father's part with success. Thus the brothers had no alternative, if they were to live together, but—not, perhaps, until they had passed through many dangerous crises—to institute the law against incest, by which they all alike renounced the women whom they desired and who had been their chief motive for despatching their father [their mother and sisters—G. M.].[38]

Commentators on this reconstruction of the supposedly phylogenetic event which Freud referred to as his "scientific myth" have established clearly how allegorical it is of the psychoanalytic movement over which Freud presided.[39] Though we may challenge Freud's conviction that the primal crime is the Rosetta Stone by which mythology in general may be explicated, there is no questioning the heuristic value of the story in explicating the relationship of Freud to his followers. Like the primal father of whom he wrote in *Totem and Taboo*, Freud was notoriously authoritarian in his dealings with his colleagues. In this connection, one thinks immediately of Adler, the first of a number of talented early analysts to be driven out from the Psychoanalytic Association in retribution for advancing theories that deviated too greatly from those that Freud held to be sacrosanct. When Jung began to delve into mythology, an area hitherto unexplored by Freud, Freud began to experience something of the jealousy of the primal father and felt compelled to make his seminal contribution to this area before Jung could. The tyranny inspiring this pre-emptive strike that Freud had launched with his swifter pen did not fail to rankle with Jung, who had, by then, come to regard Freud, as he told him in a letter, as "a dangerous rival."[40]

Like Óðinn plunging his sword so deeply into Barnstock that none save its intended heir could draw it free, Freud in *Totem and Taboo* took in hand all that he had previously discovered about infantile sexuality from his reconstruction of the ontogenetic development of contemporary neurotics and thrust it deeply into the prehistory of mankind, showing

---

[38] Freud, *Totem and Taboo*, p. 144.
[39] George Hogenson, *Jung's Struggle with Freud* (Wilmette, IL: Chiron Publications, 1994), pp. 142-145.
[40] McGuire, ed. *The Freud/Jung Letters*, p. 490.

how it may be found there as well. In pointed contrast to Jung, whose foray into mythology was leading him away from strict adherence to established sexual theory, Freud argued that our archaic forebears, too, were subject to the triadic vicissitudes of the Oedipus complex even if their myths and religious practices, like contemporary dreams, obscured this fact. While he fully agreed with Jung in positing a collective mind composed of phylogenetic schemas,[41] he felt that these schemas did little more than predispose the child to experience what it would experience anyway, its sexuality and triadic family milieu being what they were. In effect, Freud's acknowledgement of a collective mind served merely to reiterate his belief in the centrality of infantile sexuality in the life of the psyche. Far from being a spiritual factor constituted of timeless themes that might lead the individual beyond the family to later stages of development, as Jung was coming to believe, the phylogenetic unconscious was, for Freud, a template of familial patterns acquired by children during their *early* relations with parents through countless generations. Had Freud been willing to grant a greater measure of importance to the subsequent stages of ontogenetic development, as Jung did, he might have been able to tolerate Jung's wider view of the phylogenetic unconscious as well. This, however, he could not do.[42]

---

[41] Sigmund Freud, "From the History of an Infantile Neurosis," *Collected Papers* vol. III: 473-605. tr. A. & J. Strachey (London: The Hogarth Press & The Institute of Psycho-Analysis, 1950), p. 578.

[42] Cf. Freud, "From the History of an Infantile Neurosis." A passage from this text, written after the break with Jung, substantiates this assertion: "I am inclined to take the view that [phylogenetically inherited schemas] are precipitates from the history of human civilization. The Oedipus complex ... is the best known member of the class. Wherever experiences fail to fit in with the hereditary schema, they become remodelled in the imagination. ... We are often able to see the schema triumphing over the experience of the individual; as when in our present case the boy's father became the castrator and the menace to his infantile sexuality ..." (p. 603). Because both the phylogenetic schema and the ontogenetic experience have the same content for Freud, the process simultaneously works the other way as well: given all that he has said about hereditary schemas, "the significance of the traumas of early childhood ... lie[s] in the fact that to this [phylogenetic] unconscious they would contribute material which would save it from being worn away by the subsequent course of development" (p. 604). Of course, what Freud here vaguely refers to as "the subsequent course of development" corresponds to what Jung calls the current adaptational challenge of adolescent and post-adolescent development. That the unconscious might also have phylogenetic schemata prospectively related to these conflicts and life-stages is a prospect which Freud disregards. Freud's failure to do justice to Jung's position in this regard provides a vantage point for a critique of the order of precedence he prescribes concerning phylogenetic explanation. Railing against Jung for "obstinately disputing the importance of infantile prehistory while at the same time freely acknowledging the importance of ancestral prehistory," Freud declared that he "regard[ed] it as a methodological error to seize upon

Freud's Sword in Jung's Hands

> My heroic attitude *toward the world* was never a secret to
> me, from earliest childhood on; I would have known it even
> without analysis. Without your instruction I would have
> believed, like all laymen, that I was dreaming of Siegfried,
> since I am always dwelling on heroic fantasies. ... I violently
> resisted the interpretation of Siegfried as a real child, *and
> on the basis of my mystical tendencies* I would have simply
> thought that a great and heroic destiny awaited me, that I
> had to sacrifice myself for the creation of something great.
> How else could I interpret those dreams in which my father
> or grandfather blessed me and said, "A great destiny awaits
> you, my child"?[43]
>
> —Sabina Spielrein, Letter to Jung, January 19, 1918

If it had been Siggeur's prerogative to draw the sword from
Barnstock, Jung might well have retained his original position in
the psychoanalytic movement—that of Freud's adopted son and heir.
The archetypal dynamics of the situation being what they were,
however, Jung could no more wield the sword Freud wished to pass
on to him as his own than Siggeur could draw the sword from the
tree in our saga. This was not for lack of trying. In the early years of
his association with the psychoanalytic movement Jung was an ardent
champion of Freud's views. The exogamous libido he invested in this
extroverted pursuit, however, was at the same time inwardly
compensated for by a more endogamous, or as he conceptualized it at
the time, "introverted" current of libido. That this was so was already
evident in Jung's analysis of Spielrein. Though he began the analysis
in line with the theories of Freud's he wished to test, he quickly found
that his patient's condition worsened. Resisting her doctor's
interpretations, Spielrein replaced her presenting neurosis with a
transference neurosis that had a strongly inductive effect upon him.

---

phylogenetic explanation before ontogenetic possibilities have been exhausted" (p. 578).
From a Jungian point of view, it is only because Freud disputed the significance
of adolescent and post-adolescent development stressed by Jung that Jung appeared
to him to be guilty of this error of shortchanging ontogenetic possibilities in favour of
phylogenetic explanation.
    [43] Cited in Carotenuto, *A Secret Symmetry*, pp. 79-80.

At this juncture, Jung did what the mythical hero he would soon write about in his *Wandlungen* was purported to have done: having reached an impasse in his own adaptation, even as his patient had in hers, he regressed into his own depths, the depths of the mother, as these were projected onto Spielrein (who had done much the same herself with respect to Jung) for rebirth. At this point, Siggeur gave way to Sigmund in the archetypal foreground of Jung's life.

The regression Jung experienced during his work with Spielrein was partly theoretical. Unable to stay the course with his application of Freudian ideas (possibly because as a novice he had been applying them too wildly), Jung returned to the ideas and perspectives that had concerned him during the pre-Freudian period of his doctoral dissertation—parapsychology, astrology, and the occult. In the course of studying the partial personalities of his medium-cousin Helene Preiswerk for his dissertation, Jung had come to the view that at least one of these personalities was a latent form of the young woman's future adult adaptation.[44] This was essentially the same interpretation he eventually gave to Spielrein (or she to him).[45] The son, "Siegfried," whom she believed it was her fate to conceive with Jung, far from being an actual child (as Jung's earlier Freudian interpretations had suggested), was symbolic of her own heroic destiny.

---

[44] Jung, *CW* 1 § 116. "The patient pours her own soul into the role of the Clairvoyante, seeking to create out of it an ideal of virtue and perfection; she anticipates her own future and embodies in [the partial personality or imaginal figure of] Ivenes what she wishes to be in twenty years' time—the assured, influential, wise, gracious, pious lady."

[45] Cf. Carotenuto, *A Secret Symmetry*, pp. 105-106. Writing to Freud about Jung on June 30, 1909, Spielrein states: "In conversation and also in a letter Dr. Jung identifies me with his mother, and I him—with my brother and father .... In the course of an analysis it turned out that so-and-so many years ago Dr. Jung had been fond of a dark-haired hysterical girl called S.W., who always described herself as Jewish (but in reality was not.) ... Dr. Jung and I were very good at reading each other's minds. But suddenly he gets terribly worked up, gives me his diary, and says mockingly that I should open it at random, since I am so wise and know how to find my fortune. I open it—and lo and behold! it was the very passage where S.W. appeared to Dr. Jung one night in a white garment. I believe it is the only place in the entire book where he mentions this girl. ... This girl was deeply rooted in him, and she was my prototype. ... [R]ight at the beginning of my therapy Dr. Jung let me read his dissertation, in which he described this S.W. Later on he would sometimes turn reflective when I said something to him; such and such a woman had spoken in just this way, etc. And it was always this girl!" Spielrein goes on to discuss Jung's attraction to Freud's daughter and how this is another, and to her more preferable, background to Jung's transference to herself. Claiming the existence of a "psychic kinship" between herself and Freud's daughter, Spielrein thereby links herself to Freud.

The other aspect of Jung's regression implicated him more personally. Though Jung writes in his autobiography that Spielrein was referred to him by another doctor, who had "acquired a transference to her and finally begged her not to come to him any more, for if she did, it would mean the destruction of his marriage,"[46] this doctor, as Kerr has shown, was none other than Jung himself.[47] Compelled to love in Spielrein what he had, in his allegiance to Freud, denied of his own personal equation (that is, his creative link to the ancestral soul), Jung became increasingly bound to her, the more he attempted to apply Freud's principles to her treatment. Expressed in the language of our saga, no sooner had Jung become a Siggeur in relation to his own soul than his soul, projected into Spielrein's, appeared to him, as Signy had appeared to her brother Sigmund when she sought him out in his forest hideout, there to conceive with him incestuously a child of doubly Hun blood who would avenge the murder of her father and brothers. If Jung as a Freudian was unable to eradicate his patient's incest fantasy, it was because in a deeper sense, this fantasy, in which he partook on a very deep level, was pregnant with his own post-Freudian self. Complementary to the hero of Jung's *Wandlungen*, who becomes his own father, Spielrein, as Kerr has argued, played for Jung the role of dual-mother, that destructive but also creative incestuous matrix to which the hero returns for rebirth.[48] As Spielrein simply (and yet not so simply) insisted, Siegfried was not only the child she would have with Jung, but at the same time Jung himself. This was so, regardless of whether or not she accepted Jung's symbolic interpretation (which, in fact, she basically did).

Jung Draws the Sword

> Every sexual symbol in a dream, as in mythology, possesses the significance of a life- and death-bringing god.[49]
>
> —Sabina Spielrein

In ancient times the feeling of being "penetrated" by, or of "receiving," the god was allegorized by the sexual act. But it

---

[46] Jung, *Memories, Dreams, Reflections*, p. 138.
[47] Kerr, *A Most Dangerous Method*, p. 311.
[48] Kerr, *A Most Dangerous Method*, p. 333.
[49] Sabina Spielrein, "Destruction as a Cause of Coming into Being" (1912), *The Journal of Analytical Psychology* 39.2 (1994): 157.

would be a gross misunderstanding to interpret a genuine religious experience as a "repressed" sexual fantasy on account of a mere metaphor. The "penetration" can also be expressed by a sword, spear, or arrow.[50]

—C. G. Jung

J ung's writings abound with passages in which we may witness him drawing the sword from Barnstock. In his concepts of *participation mystique*, the parental imago, and introversion we can already sense the heft of the sword's handle in his hand. Sigmund's sword Gram, in Jung's thought, is neither the Oedipal threat posed by one's actual father nor the castrating blade of the primal father. On the contrary, it is a representation of the age-old psychic factor, the libido, or life-force, which the dependent child, projecting outward all that it is unconscious of in itself, first experiences in the form of the life-giving (death dealing) power of the parents, and then later, in the heroic, consciousness-creating adolescent phase of life, wrests free from the parents and makes its own.

Also illustrative of this decisive shift in Jung's thought is a passage from the preface to the third edition of his paper, "The Significance of the Father in the Destiny of the Individual."[51] In this passage Jung, employing images similar to those that are central to our saga, explains the shift in perspective which necessitated the revisions that appear in this final version of his paper. With the image of Gram in the trunk of Barnstock in mind, let us observe how Jung, enacting the drama inherent in these images, wrests the razor-edged sword of his own mature viewpoint free from the theories of Freud in which it had previously been lodged:

> Experience in later years has … altered and deepened many things. … I have seen how the roots of the psyche and of fate go deeper than the "family romance," and that not only the children but the parents, too, are merely branches of one great tree. While I was working on the mother-complex in my book *Wandlungen und Symbole der Libido*, it became clear to me what the deeper causes of this complex are; why not only the father, but the mother as well, is such an important factor in the child's fate: not because they themselves have this or that human failing or merit, but because they happen

---

[50] Jung, *CW* 10 § 638.
[51] Jung, *CW* 4, pages 301-322.

to be—by accident, so to speak—the human beings who first
impress on the childish mind those mysterious and mighty
laws which govern not only families but entire nations,
indeed the whole of humanity. Not laws devised by wit of
man, but the laws and forces of nature, amongst which man
walks as on the edge of a razor.[52]

Worth quoting here are several passages from Jung's writings that
may be read both as amplifications of this passage and as further examples
of how Jung's thought enacts the images of our Northern saga. The first
is taken from a letter to a correspondent who sought Jung's advice
regarding her apparently tyrannical and possessive parents. Drawing on
the image of the tree, even as does our saga, Jung paradoxically upholds
the appropriateness of the child's growing resistance to its parents, not
on the grounds that such relations are incestuous and therefore taboo,
but that they are not incestuous enough (in the higher sense of the term),
and are, therefore, an affront to a deeper cathexis of kinship libido.

Parents must realize that they are trees from which the fruit
falls in the autumn. Children don't belong to their parents,
and they are only apparently produced by them. In reality
they come from a thousand-year-old stem, or rather from
many stems, and often they are about as characteristic of
their parents as an apple on a fir-tree.[53]

Our second passage is from Jung's "Introduction to Wickes's *Analyse
der Kinderseele.*" Here, what Jung referred to in the previous quotation
as "the thousand-year-old stem" that is more fateful for the child than
its parents reappears as what he calls "the infinity of the child's
preconscious soul." While reading this passage let us recall that in our
saga this factor is represented as the spirit of Óðinn, which invests each
generation of Volsung children.

The infinity of the child's preconscious soul ... [is] the
mysterious *spiritus rector* of our weightiest deeds and of our
individual destinies. ... For behind every individual father
there stands the primordial image of the Father, and behind

---

[52] Jung, *CW* 4, page 301.
[53] C. G. Jung, *Letters*, vol. I: 1906-1950 & vol. II: 1951-1961, ed. G. Adler & A.
Jaffé, tr. R. F. C. Hull (Princeton, NJ: Princeton University Press, 1973 & 1975), vol.
1, pp. 217-218.

the fleeting personal mother the magical figure of the Magna Mater. These archetypes of the collective psyche, whose power is magnified in immortal works of art and in the fiery tenets of religion, are the dominants that rule the preconscious soul of the child and, when projected upon the human parents, lend them a fascination which often assumes monstrous proportions. From that there arises the false aetiology of neurosis which, in Freud, ossified into a system: the Oedipus complex. And that is also why, in the later life of the neurotic, the images of the parents can be criticized, corrected, and reduced to human dimensions, while yet continuing to work like divine agencies. Did the human father really possess this mysterious power, his sons would soon liquidate him or, even better, would refrain from becoming fathers themselves. ... Far better to leave this sovereign power to the gods, with whom it had always rested before man became "enlightened."[54]

What Jung says concerning the individual father becoming the bearer for his children of the power of the archetype applies as well to the Freud-Jung relationship. During the period of his sonship to Freud, Jung, like the children he discusses in this passage, projected this power onto Freud. With his recognition that the power of the father is a function of the archetype, however, Jung resolved what he called his "'religious' crush"[55] on the older man. Expressed in terms of the imagery of our saga, this recognition was equivalent to Sigmund's drawing the sword from the trunk of Barnstock. Having identified with the paternal archetype, Freud experienced the change in Jung's outlook as being motivated by parricidal wishes. For Jung, however, withdrawing this projection was essentially an act of sacrifice. In differentiating between the father archetype and its incidental human bearer, Jung sacrificed his childish dependence on Freud and became heir to the "infinity of the child's preconscious soul," that "thousand-year-old stem," on a more conscious, adult level.[56]

---

[54] Jung, *CW* 17 § 97.

[55] McGuire, ed. *The Freud/Jung Letters*, p. 95.

[56] From Jung's post-Freudian point of view, Freud's theoretical fantasy of a primal crime of parricide was compensatory to his identification with the father archetype. Unable to sacrifice his relationship to the infantile objects he studied, Freud clung to them in his theories. In this way he foreclosed recognition of the significance of the archetypal psyche and became, as he described himself, "a godless Jew." Jung makes his view of this clear in a letter to Spielrein, which was part of a late exchange between the two in which they enacted something of the deep, identity-renewing incest of

> The fantasy of sacrifice means the giving up of infantile wishes. ... The chief obstacle to new modes of psychological adaptation is conservative adherence to the earlier attitude. But man cannot leave his previous personality and his previous objects of interest simply as they are, otherwise his libido would stagnate in the past .... Here religion is a great help because, by the bridge of the symbol, it leads his libido away from the infantile objects (parents) towards the symbolic representative of the past, i.e., the gods, thus facilitating the transition from the infantile world to the adult world. In this way the libido is set free for social purposes.[57]

What Freud interpreted as the primordial father's incest-thwarting castration threat, Jung, by contrast, interpreted as the son's necessary sacrifice of an attitude which, having passed beyond the zenith of its adaptive potential, must be allowed to descend through the so-called "incest barrier" to the depths of ancestral soul for renewal, even as the sun descends beneath the sea so as to rise again the following day. As a conceptual enactment of what our saga images as Sigmund's drawing the sword out of Barnstock, Jung's prospective, post-Freudian reading of castration as sacrifice and incest as rebirth is in keeping with the nature of the god who thrust the sword into that tree in the first place. Like the sword he brings, all-father Óðinn was also impaled upon a tree as a sacrifice. For nine days, it is said, he hung suspended by a spear on the trunk of Yggdrasill, "a sacrifice of myself to myself."[58] Just as a gardener stimulates a tree or shrub to flourish by pruning it, so the psyche seeks to renew itself, incestuously from its deepest root, by sacrificing spindly branches. Significantly, even one's literal parents are spindly branches in comparison with this great, ancestral root to which we all must sacrifice if we are to grow from our true depths.

The incest taboo, which produces estrangement between family members and leads ultimately to the diminishment of family ties, is a

---

Sigmund and Signy: "Do not forget that the Jews also had prophets. You do not yet live one part of the Jewish soul because you look too much to the external. That is— regrettably—the curse of the Jew: his innermost and deepest soul he calls 'infantile wish fulfillment.' He murders his own prophet, murders even his Messiah." Cited in Kerr, *A Most Dangerous Method*, p. 486. For a different translation of the letter from which this passage is taken see C. G. Jung, "The Letters of C. G. Jung to Sabina Spielrein," tr. B. Wharton, *The Journal of Analytical Psychology* 46.1 (2001): 192.

[57] Jung, *CW* 4 § 350.
[58] From the *Hávamál* of the *Elder Edda*, stanza 138.

function of a deeper, archetypal incest prerogative. It is because we are more like the thousand-year-old stem than we are like our parents that we feel compelled to leave our parents for partners outside the family. Of course, few people differentiate themselves so completely from their *participation mystique* with their parents that there remains no trace of parental influence in their choice of love object. But as Jung says, "It is normal that children should in a certain sense marry their parents. This is just as important, psychologically, as the biological necessity to infuse new blood if the ancestral tree is to produce a good breed. It guarantees continuity, a reasonable prolongation of the past into the present. Only too much or too little in this direction is harmful."[59] The sword of incest cuts both ways: not only does it inhibit incest, it also requires it.

One of Jung's most sword-brandishing statements regarding the psychological significance of the incest fantasy appears in his paper, "The Psychology of the Transference." The excerpt that appears below was written to elucidate a woodcut in the series from the *Rosarium Philosophorum*, which Jung believed depicted the objective (that is, archetypal) dimension of the transference. This particular woodcut bears images analogous to those in our saga. Indeed, just as Óðinn's namesake Signy marries Siggeur beneath the branches of Barnstock, only to commit incest subsequently with her brother Sigmund, so in this picture from the *Rosarium*, the divine siblings, Apollo and Diana, hold hands in incestuous matrimony while extending branches toward each other with their free hands. And just as in our saga the god Óðinn appears with his sword and plunges it into the trunk of Barnstock, so in this *Rosarium* woodcut the Holy Ghost descends from a star in the form of a dove bearing in its beak a branch which intersects with the branches held by the couple.

> ... [T]he intervention of the Holy Ghost reveals the hidden meaning of the incest, whether of brother and sister or of mother and son, as a repulsive symbol for the *unio mystica*. ... Incest symbolizes union with one's own being, it means individuation or becoming a self, and, because this is so vitally important, it exerts an unholy fascination—not, perhaps, as a crude reality, but certainly as a psychic process controlled by the unconscious .... It is for this reason, and not because of occasional cases of human incest, that the

---

[59] Jung, *CW* 10 § 73.

first gods were believed to propagate their kind
incestuously. Incest is simply the union of like with like,
which is the next stage in the development of the primitive
idea of self-fertilization.[60]

Though Jung wrote the essay from which this passage is taken
relatively late in his career (and dedicated it to his wife, Emma), the
interpretation of incest he sets out in it is consistent with the
interpretation he and Spielrein came to at the beginning of his career,
once he had appreciated the prospective meaning of her resistance to his
literalistic, Freudian approach to her fantasy of having his child. Spanning
these diametrically opposed relationships (wife and patient), the essay is
both a full theoretical account of the prospective meaning of transference-
countertransference phenomena, such as those which led him into such
deep waters with Spielrein, as well as the "psychotherapeutic handbook
for gentlemen"[61] that Emma Jung had suggested that she might have to
write during those erotically turbulent early years. In this connection,
and in connection to the previous quotation about the critical balance
between the need for continuity with the parents and the need for new
blood, let us recall that Jung told Spielrein, in the midst of their psyche-
plumbing venture together, that he loved her on account of the
"remarkable parallelism of [their] thoughts ... and her magnificent proud
character ... [but] would never marry her because he harbour[ed] within
himself a great philistine who craves narrow limits and the typical Swiss
style."[62] For Jung, the incestuous union with oneself is a dialectical
product of endogamous and exogamous energic trends, a delicate and
oscillating balance of mother and anima, wife and mistress, polygamy
and the typical Swiss style. "Only too much or too little in this direction
[or that direction] is harmful."

If we apply the principle of extensity to Jung's thought,[63] we should
expect to find a carryover of the incest theme into other ideas. We have
already seen the role incest played in his late statement about the
psychology of the transference. Another instance of carryover might be

---

[60] Jung, *CW* 16 § 419.
[61] McGuire, ed. *The Freud/Jung Letters*, p. 72.
[62] Cited in Kerr, *A Most Dangerous Method*, p. 312.
[63] Jung, *CW* 8 § 38. Extensity refers to a characteristic of psychic energy
transformation wherein "libido does not leave a structure as pure intensity and pass
without trace into another, but ... takes the character of the old function over into
the new."

seen in an early paper, written at a time when Jung was just coming out of the turmoil occasioned by the break with Freud and the renunciation of Spielrein. Titled "The Transcendent Function," this paper is less concerned with describing the transference than with outlining a means of facilitating its resolution. Whereas in his earlier writings, such as *Wandlungen*, Jung had sought to re-interpret incest, in this paper he incestuously reconceived the nature of psychoanalytic interpretation itself. Just as he had learned through his work with Spielrein of the inefficacy of interpreting imaginal figures such as Siegfried reductively, so in this essay he argues that there is a stage in analysis at which "dissolution of the symbol ... is a mistake."[64] Symbols, as Jung came to realize, cannot be reduced to infantile sexuality without remainder. In fact, the symbolic significance of the remainder is so immense that Jung recognized in it the bridge to something more: the patient's potential for adaptation to his or her current adult life and future destiny.[65]

The interpretive stance born of this recognition Jung called constructive-synthetic interpretation. To illustrate its use, Jung, significantly enough, discusses the dream of an unmarried female patient, "who dreamt that *someone gave her a wonderful, richly ornamented, antique sword dug up out of a tumulus.*"[66] The sword in the dream reminded the dreamer of her father's dagger, which he had once flashed in the sun, and of her father's impetuous temperament and adventurous love life. As well, it recalled her Celtic ancestry, of which she was proud. For the sake of contrast and comparison, Jung provides the Freudian (or, as he calls it, "analytical") interpretation, before tendering for discussion his new "constructive" interpretation. Keeping in mind that Jung, as a Freudian psychoanalyst and president of the International Psychoanalytic Association, had himself made such interpretations in the early phase of his analysis of Spielrein, let us quote Jung's rendition of a Freudian reading of the dream:

---

[64] Jung, *CW* 8 § 148.

[65] Jung, *Letters*, vol. 1, pp. 142-143: "Behind all the rationalizations of Freud's theory there are still facts that need to be understood. It is futile to devalue them with the famous 'nothing but' formula. If in exceptional cases the inner demand can be reduced to silence, people have lost something and they pay for their apparent calm with inner desiccation. The irrational factors that manifest themselves indirectly as 'incest complexes' and 'infantile fantasies,' etc., are susceptible of a quite different interpretation."

[66] Jung, *CW* 8 § 149.

> Patient has a pronounced father complex and a rich tissue of
> sexual fantasies about her father, whom she lost early. She always
> put herself in her mother's place, although with strong
> resistances towards her father. She has never been able to
> accept a man like her father and has therefore chosen weakly,
> neurotic men against her will. Also in the analysis violent
> resistance towards the physician-father. The dream digs up
> her wish for her father's "weapon." The rest is clear. In
> theory, this would immediately point to a phallic fantasy.[67]

Side by side with this "analytical interpretation," Jung places his
"constructive interpretation." If the analytical reading is comparable to
the sword of Óðinn lodged in the trunk of Barnstock, the constructive
reading is comparable to Sigmund's drawing it forth:

> It is as if the patient needed such a weapon. Her father had
> the weapon. He was energetic, lived accordingly, and also
> took upon himself the difficulties inherent in his
> temperament. Therefore, though living a passionate, exciting
> life he was not neurotic. This weapon is a very ancient
> heritage of mankind, which lay buried in the patient and
> was brought to light through excavation (analysis). The
> weapon has to do with insight, with wisdom. It is a means
> of attack and defence. Her father's weapon was a passionate,
> unbending will, with which he made his way through life.
> Up till now the patient has been the opposite in every
> respect. She is just on the point of realizing that a person
> can also will something and need not merely be driven, as
> she had always believed. The will based on a knowledge of
> life and on insight is an ancient heritage of the human race,
> which also is in her, but till now lay buried, for in this
> respect, too, she is her father's daughter. But she had not
> appreciated this till now, because her character had been that
> of a perpetually whining, pampered, spoilt child. She was
> extremely passive and completely given to sexual fantasies.[68]

Constructive interpretation is rooted in the new interpretation of
incest that Jung arrived at in *Wandlungen*. Just as Goethe, Jung's legendary
forefather, wrote, "What thou hast inherited from thy fathers, acquire it

---

[67] Jung, *CW* 8, page 76.
[68] Jung, *CW* 8, page 76.

to make it thine,"[69] so Jung's constructive stance with respect to interpretation invites the dreamer to recognize the potential of her ancestral soul and make its possibilities actual in her own life. Interpretation in this sense is itself an enactment of a higher incest. Conceived as a constructive union with the deepest roots of one's being, the rhizome from which life springs, constructive interpretation transcends the lower incest, which ties the neurotic to the analyst as if to a parent—hence the associated notion of a transcendent function. Expressed in the language of our saga, constructive interpretation effects a union with the forefathers (in whose line Óðinn repeatedly invests himself) and thereby draws out the sword. Just as Óðinn plunges his sword into Barnstock and Sigmund, his great-great-grandson, draws it free, so every act of interpretation that turns reflexively upon itself in the recognition that it, too, is a fantasy production of the psyche incestuously reinvests itself with its own hermeneutic spirit. Said another way, each time a symbol is hallowed as the best approximation of something unknown and named accordingly (i.e., by the name of the more unknown, and finally by the name of God[70]), Óðinn—that self-sacrificing root of the objective psyche which turns upon itself in the form of a sword—once again infuses life into our psychic growth process.

Spielrein's Fetch

> A tree sprouting from a seed resembles its species, but is not identical with every other tree. Whether we perceive a continuation or a disappearance of the former content emphasized in the new product is a subjective matter.[71]
>
> — Sabina Spielrein

Sexual maturity brings with it the possibility of a new personal *participation mystique*, and hence of replacing that part of the personality which was lost in identification with the parents. A new archetype is constellated: in a man it is the archetype of woman, and in a woman the archetype of man. These two figures were likewise hidden behind the

---

[69] Cited in Sigmund Freud, *An Outline of Psychoanalysis*, tr. J. Strachey (New York: W. W. Norton, 1963), p. 123.
[70] Jung, *Memories, Dreams, Reflections*, p. 354.
[71] Spielrein, "Destruction as a Cause of Coming into Being," p. 163.

mask of the parental imagos, but now they step forth
undisguised, even though strongly influenced by the parental
imagos, often overwhelmingly so. I have given the feminine
archetype in man the name "anima," and the masculine
archetype in woman the name "animus,"....[72]

— C. G. Jung

In a passage of his memoirs, the octogenarian Jung records the earliest
recollection of his life. As this recollection has to do with Jung's infant
self, we may be put in mind by it of the prospective reading that he and
Spielrein eventually gave to Spielrein's fantasy of giving him a little son
and of his actually being her son.[73]

> I am lying in a pram, in the shadow of a tree. It is a fine,
> warm summer day, the sky blue, and golden sunlight darting
> through green leaves. The hood of the pram has been left
> up. I have just awakened to the glorious beauty of the day,
> and have a sense of indescribable well-being. I see the sun
> glittering through the leaves and blossoms of the bushes.
> Everything is wholly wonderful, colorful and splendid.[74]

Jung in his pram in the shadow of a tree is the incestuously conceived
son of the Northern child-trunk, Barnstock, even as Adonis was the
incestuous progeny of a Mediterranean tree. The golden sunlight darting
through the green leaves is emblematic, likewise, of the sword-like
consciousness to which Jung became heir through his incestuous union
with himself in his patient Spielrein. Wielding this sword, Jung, loyal to
the promptings of the heretical blood that coursed through his veins,
sacrificed his filial tie to Freud even as Spielrein sacrificed the infantile
tie to her parents.

Prospectively considered, this deepening of the transference-
countertransference neurosis corresponded to a shrinking of the parental
imagos and the establishment of "a new personal *participation mystique*"
between doctor and patient, one which replaced that part of each of
their personalities which had been lost through their former identification with

---

[72] Jung, *CW* 10 § 71.
[73] Jung and Spielrein returned to a discussion of Spielrein's Siegfried fantasy in an
exchange of letters years after their work together in analysis had ended. See C. G.
Jung, "The Letters of C. G. Jung to Sabina Spielrein," tr. B. Wharton, *The Journal of
Analytical Psychology* 46.1 (2001): 173-199.
[74] Jung, *Memories, Dreams, Reflections*, p. 6.

parents or parent-figures. Further differentiation of consciousness, however, would require that this new *participation mystique* be sacrificed even as Jung would sacrifice his sonship to Freud, and Spielrein her reliance on her parents. The apparent betrayal of their love may, thus, be understood to have had not only a conventional social and analytic necessity, but an archetypal one: the "internalization through sacrifice" of the anima and animus.[75]

The form that this individuation-promoting sacrifice took in Jung's life is well known. As Jung recounts in his autobiography, in the midst of his work in self-analysis after the break with Freud, he entered into conversation with a feminine voice in himself. This voice, which Jung identifies as that of "a talented psychopath who had a strong transference to him,"[76] was an interior echo of the voice of Spielrein, as Kerr has demonstrated.[77] By responding to Spielrein's voice in himself, Jung entered into dialogue with that aspect of his psyche that she had activated in him. Conversation with this asymmetrical psychic factor, which he later called the anima, brought him into more intimate relationship with himself.[78]

Spielrein's equivalent of Jung's process of actively imagining in himself what she had previously carried for him outwardly came in the writing of her seminal essay, "Destruction as a Cause of Coming into Being."[79] Drawing both on Norse mythology (via the *Niebelungenlied*) and tree symbolism (as Jung did in *Wandlungen*), Spielrein formulated in this article her own conceptual account of the process she had been through with Jung. In this way Spielrein made more consciously her own an aspect of her psychic heritage that had appeared to her first in projection as a content of her transference to Jung.

Reading this essay in the context of our Northern saga, we may hear it as a recurrence, in the language of psychoanalysis, of Signy's speech regarding the Volsung family fetch. For, just as Signy, the feminine link between the Huns and the Goths, warned her father Volsung of the spirit

---

[75] John Layard, "The Incest Taboo and the Virgin Archetype," in his *The Virgin Archetype* (New York: Spring Publications, 1972), pp. 284-288. See also Jung, *CW* 16 § 438. For an important critique of the notion see James Hillman, *Anima: An Anatomy of a Personified Notion* (Dallas: Spring Publications, 1985), pp. 115-127.
[76] Jung, *Memories, Dreams, Reflections*, p. 185.
[77] Kerr, *A Most Dangerous Method*, pp. 502-507.
[78] Jung, *Memories, Dreams, Reflections*, pp. 185-188.
[79] Spielrein, "Destruction as a Cause of Coming into Being," pp. 155-186.

in their bloodline that resists alliances such as the one that was to be established through her marriage to Siggeur, so Spielrein, the feminine link between Zürich and Vienna, combined the ideas of both Freud and Jung to write a highly original contribution of her own on the destructive aspect of sexuality. In so doing, she remained as loyal a daughter to Freud as Signy was to Volsung, while at the same time conceiving with Jung, in the manner of Signy with her bother Sigmund, the great Aryan-Semitic hero of her dreams, Siegfried.

In summary, Spielrein's theory accommodated both Freud's emphasis on sexuality and Jung's interest in the phylogenetic or mythological layer of the unconscious in order to explain the resistances that the ego feels toward sexuality. Having experienced these fetch-like resistances firsthand both in herself and in Jung, Spielrein recognized them to be a ubiquitous phenomenon, something inherent to the ego's experience of sexuality.

Simply put, in Spielrein's view, the life of the psyche is constituted of the interplay of two instincts, the instinct of species-preservation (sexuality) and the instinct of self-preservation. These instincts correspond, in turn, to two psychic structures, the ego and the unconscious. Vitalized by the instinct for self-preservation, the ego (or "I") of ordinary conscious identity exists in a relationship of conflict with the unconscious, the unconscious being vitalized by the species-oriented sexual instinct. Because sexuality cares nothing for the interests of the individual, but only wants progeny in some form (e.g., children, or artistic creations of value to the race), the ego experiences the desirous imperatives of sexuality, the desirous imperatives of the unconscious, as destructive and death-dealing, and consequently mobilizes an attitude of resistance in response. One expression of this resistance to sexuality is incestuous or incest-like attachments, for unions of this sort pose less of a threat to the ego. On the other hand, if one can tolerate the dissolution of one's ego in sexuality—if, that is to say, one can temporarily sacrifice one's egoism—one can be vitalized by the "total energy of countless generations," even as Spielrein felt herself to be vitalized by the line of Jewish religious leaders in her own ancestry.[80] This vitalizing surge of sexuality which "saturates [the ego's personal] desires with blood" is imaged in our saga as the bloody fate which befalls both the Huns and

---

[80] Carotenuto, *A Secret Symmetry*, p. 39.

the Goths.[81] It is through immersion in just such a blood bath of destructive sexual imagery that the ego receives, and is valorized by, the heroic vocation that transforms fate into destiny.[82]

Relinquishing the incestuous relationship to Jung in which had been conceived the symbol that would allow her to sacrifice herself to this species-preserving, vocation-conferring sexuality, Spielrein gave birth to her child, Siegfried, in the form of her "Destruction" paper. When Jung, in his capacity as editor of the *Jahrbuch*, read Spielrein's paper—mailed to him with a covering letter that identified it as the child of their love, Siegfried[83]—he published it side by side with Part 2 of his "Transformations and Symbols of the Libido," in recognition both of its collective value and its kinship with his own thought. Inwardly, however, this animus-emancipating achievement of the outer woman, Spielrein, may have served to deepen the conflict between Jung and his inner woman, the anima. For, in light of Jung's statement in his memoirs that what his anima said to him in his dialogues with her seemed to be "full of a deep cunning,"[84] we may surmise that Jung had become subject to resistances such as those Spielrein wrote of in her paper. Already long familiar, through the uncanny voice of his mother as well as through personality No. 2 in himself, with what Spielrein meant by sexuality, Jung strove to hold onto the *individual* character of his psyche so that the split in himself (in Spielrein's view, the *generic* split between the ego-instinct of self-preservation and sexuality) could be healed.

Jung's life task, as he characterized it in one of his letters, was "to climb down a thousand ladders until I could reach out my hand to the little clod of earth that I am."[85] Ever leery of losing his individual identity to a collective representation, the sword-brandishing Jung learned to differentiate himself from such identifications by personifying them in imaginal dialogues. Read from the point of view of Spielrein's paper, the various figures from which Jung derived his conceptual model of the relations between the ego and the unconscious—persona, shadow, anima, wise-old-man and the self—might be seen as resistances to sexuality. Read from their own inherent point of view, however, they are attempts to turn

---

[81] Carotenuto, *A Secret Symmetry*, p. 70.
[82] The recent Hollywood film, *Braveheart*, tells much the same tale.
[83] Carotenuto, *A Secret Symmetry*, p. 48: "Receive now the product of our love, the project which is your little son Siegfried."
[84] Jung, *Memories, Dreams, Reflections*, p. 187.
[85] Jung, *Letters*, vol. 1, p. 19.

the encounter with what Spielrein called sexuality (and Jung came to call the collective unconscious) to the advantage of both the individual and the species through the process of individuation.

In Jung's view, the ego, far from being as individually personal as Spielrein's theory assumes, is as collective as sexuality itself, until it is differentiated out from a whole series of archetypal identifications. This is why Jung, loyal to the sanguine promptings of his introverted temperament, would dissolve his personal *participation mystique* with Spielrein through active imagination, and kill in himself the Siegfried, which Spielrein then had to carry to term in herself, without him, in sublimated form. For though Spielrein might have interpreted Jung's nauseating dream of a blond-haired youth with a wound in his head floating past him in a stream of blood as a representation of his ego's fear of their great love, Jung, after a subsequent dream in which he killed the mythical figure Siegfried, interpreted these dreams as heralding the sacrifice of his identification with the heroic ideals of the German peoples, which no longer suited him.[86] Having sacrificed these ideals, Jung was no longer compelled by the compensatory imperatives of his unconscious to love a dark Jewish girl. Having given back to the unconscious the "love of S. for J." that had shown him a truth that would have driven him mad had he been unable to sublimate it,[87] Jung released into his own Self-incarnating individuation process the very Semitic blood from which he, like Signy in her marriage to Siggeur, had recoiled from in Freud.[88] Reminding Spielrein that the Jews also had prophets,[89] and railing against Freud for cutting off the root of that thousand-year-old tree that links all peoples by reducing it to "infantile sexuality," Jung arrived at a vision of the psyche in which

---

[86] Jung, *Memories, Dreams, Reflections*, pp. 179-180.

[87] Jung wrote to Spielrein, September 1, 1919: "The love of S. for J. made the latter aware of something he had previously only vaguely suspected, that is, of a power in the unconscious that shapes one's destiny, a power which later led him to things of greatest importance. The relationship had to be 'sublimated' because otherwise it would have led him to delusion and madness (the concretization of the unconscious). Occasionally one must be unworthy, simply in order to be able to continue living." Cited in Kerr, *A Most Dangerous Method*, p. 491. For a different translation of the letter from which this passage is taken see C. G. Jung, "The Letters of C. G. Jung to Sabina Spielrein," tr. B. Wharton, *Journal of Analytical Psychology*, 46:1 (2001), p. 194.

[88] For a discussion of Jung's affinity with Jewish spirituality at a depth level see David Rosen, "If only Jung had a Rabbi," *The Journal of Analytical Psychology* 41.2 (1996): 245-256.

[89] Jung, "The Letters of C. G. Jung to Sabina Spielrein," *The Journal of Analytical Psychology* 46.1 (2001): 192. See also note 56 above.

the opposing endogamous and exogamous currents of the blood (that is, libido) are united.

The conceptual equivalent of this vision of a common blood (which not only underpins the family and racial levels of the unconscious, but sends the individuation-promoting sword which turns kin against kin as easily as it turns nation against nation), Jung later formulated as the collective unconscious. What may appear, when viewed from the perspective of social history, to have been a parting of the ways between Jung and Freud, and the betrayal by Jung of Spielrein, reveals itself, when viewed from the archetypal perspective of our saga, to be the outer expression of an inner dialectical process of integration and self-realization in all three. As Jung put it in his memoirs with respect to the inner figures of Salome and Elijah (who may be taken as asymmetrical responses of his psyche to Spielrein and Freud), "Only many years later, when I knew a great deal more than I knew then, did the connection between the old man and the young girl appear perfectly natural to me."[90]

The archetypal processes depicted in the Volsunga Saga continue to enact themselves upon the world stage in our own day. Perpetrating horror on a colossal scale, the Wotanic spirit that raged through Europe to the four corners of the globe during the First and Second World Wars has again and again planted its sword of incest into the tree of life, most recently in the former Yugoslavia. True to its characterization as "a most dangerous method,"[91] psychoanalysis (as I have been attempting to demonstrate in these pages) has been subject to these same archetypal powers from its very inception. That Jung, Freud, and Spielrein were able to contain as well as they did what was exploding in the outer world in bombs during their day is remarkable. Though the world remains rife with ethnic conflict, their approach to these issues has advanced our saga's plot beyond the eschaton of its failed *coniunctio*. For while the couples in the saga could never overcome the fetch of their familial and ethnic loyalties, Freud, in his discovery of the transference, and Jung in his prospective treatment of it, created an entirely new vessel of relationship: the transference-countertransference neurosis of the talking cure. Analysis by means of the consciousness created in this new form of relationship

---

[90] Jung, *Memories, Dreams, Reflections*, p. 182.
[91] In a letter to Théodore Flournoy (28 September, 1909), William James writes of psychoanalysis as "a most dangerous method" due to its emphasis on symbolism. Cited in Kerr, *A Most Dangerous Method*, p. vi.

has provided, however unwittingly, a container for the blood-complex from which history pours forth as from a haemorrhage—a container, moreover, that aims at transformation. On the way to becoming one, the two (analyst and analysand) suffer the saga of the many. And this, too, Jung came to see as only a transitional stage of diminished *participation mystique* between archaic identity and individuation, for in the final analysis it is "the individual ... [who] is the makeweight that tips the [world's] scales ...."[92]

Jung considered it a characteristic of the collective unconscious that what is truly accomplished somewhere once by someone is simultaneously accomplished everywhere for all.[93] With the dissolution of the personal *participation mystique* through which Jung and Spielrein had been unconsciously identified (i.e., the internalization through sacrifice of the anima/animus[94]), the sword-struck family tree in which all our lives are rooted became more consciously what it always already potentially was: a tree of individuation—or the dark precursor of such a tree.

Because the Signy and Sigmund of Jung's thought (the anima and animus) are mediating figures that relate us to the collective unconscious in a manner that provides for our individuation (when we do not identify with them),[95] the full significance of Jung's and Spielrein's prospective interpretation of their relationship is evident only when viewed in cultural perspective. Simply put, what Jung and Spielrein, as the progeny of Barnstock, accomplished through the sacrifice of their outer relationship, Nazi Germany failed to accomplish through its fantasy of racial supremacy and world conquest. And if today we are still subject, through that historic failure, to the mythic imperatives of Barnstock and Gram, it is because we, the heirs of Freud, Jung, and Sabina Spielrein, have yet to recognize the fetch that makes a saga of our lives for the urge to individuation that it is.

---

[92] Jung, *CW* 10 § 586.

[93] Jung, *Letters*, vol. 1, p. 58.

[94] Jung, *CW* 7 § 387: "The immediate goal of the analysis of the unconscious, therefore, is to reach a state where the unconscious contents no longer remain unconscious and no longer express themselves indirectly as animus and anima phenomena; that is to say, a state in which animus and anima become functions of relationship to the unconscious." In this passage we see Jung's formula for working through what, in another context, he called "...that unmistakable sexual obsession which shows itself whenever a patient has reached the point where he needs to be forced or tempted out of a wrong attitude or situation" (*CW* 4 § 780).

[95] Jung, *CW* 7 § 339, 521; *CW* § 9, ii § 20n1; *CW* 10 § 714; *CW* 11 § 107; *CW* 13 § 62; *CW* 18 § 187.

CHAPTER THREE

Baldr's Death: Individuation and the Ancestral Soul

The Æsir making sport of shooting Baldr

Long ago [man] formed an ideal conception of omnipotence and omniscience which he embodied in his gods. To these gods he attributed everything that seemed unattainable to his wishes, or that was forbidden to him. One may say, therefore, that these gods were cultural ideals.

—Sigmund Freud, *Civilization and its Discontents*, p. 280

When ... we make use of the concept of a God we are simply formulating a definite psychological fact, namely the independence and sovereignty of certain psychic contents which express themselves by their power to thwart our will, to obsess our consciousness, and to influence our moods and actions.

—C. G. Jung, *CW* 7 § 400

Runic Preamble

One story leads to another story and to another still. In this, our final chapter, we repeat for a third time the experiment which Jung's characterization of psychology as an archaic myth in modern dress had inspired us to carry out in the previous two chapters. Shifting the lens of our runic kaleidoscope to the purview of another Norse god, we once again expect to find, among the newly positioned colours and shapes, concepts and theories of our analytic tradition, the depth psychological equivalent of yet another of those just-so stories which the Norse myths tell about life. Baldr, the Æsir deity through whom we shall be imagining the thought of Freud and Jung in the pages that follow is a youthful god. The whitest and most beautiful of the Æsir, bright and luminous with light, he is especially beloved by his fellow gods. Little more than this, however, is known about him in our day. Indeed, as one scholar of the ancient North has commented, there exist so few descriptions of Baldr that "he would have little interest were it not for the story of his death, to which allusion is made frequently by Northern writers."[1] In turning to the tale of Baldr's dreams and death we shall be making a similar claim with respect to the concepts of psychoanalysis and analytical psychology. They, too, we hold to be of less interest in and of themselves than the drama they enact together when viewed through the lens of myth.

The Northern Myth

There are two vastly differing accounts of Baldr's death in the Norse canon. The richer of these was written by Snorri Sturluson who based his version on West Norse sources. The other account, based on East Norse sources, is that of Saxo Grammaticus. In Snorri's account, Baldr is the passive, benign deity whose features we have already briefly described. In Saxo's account he is a forceful, demigod warrior, who competes with a mortal man for the love of a woman.[2]

According to the version of the myth compiled by Snorri, Baldr, the son of Óðinn and Frigg, was troubled in the night by disturbing dreams in which his life was threatened. Hearing of these dreams, the other gods were troubled as well. Not only was Baldr the most beloved among them, but the possibility that he might be subject to death, despite his being a god, did not augur well for their immortality either. Were not such dreams as Baldr's a portent of the Ragnarök, the end of the gods? Saddling his eight-legged mount Sleipnir, Óðinn rode straight to Nivlheim (the realm of ice and cold), and on from there to Hel, which lay beyond that realm. Disguising his identity, he then consulted a seeress or Volva, who lay in a burial mound, regarding Baldr's fate. "For Baldr the mead, that noble drink, is ready brewed," the Volva told him. "And the gods," she added, "are now in great peril." Wishing to know more, Óðinn pressed the Volva to answer another question. "Who will be the bane of Baldr?" he asked. "Hod shall bring the noble hero here," the spectre replied. "And who will punish Hod for his crime?" "Rind, will give birth to Vale. At only one night old, he shall kill Baldr's slayer." At this juncture, the Volva recognized that it was Óðinn who was her interrogator and Óðinn recognized that the Volva was the one known

---

[1] E. O. G. Turville-Petre, *Myth and Religion of the North: The Religion of Ancient Scandinavia* (Westport: Greenwood Press, 1975), p. 106.

[2] For a discussion of Saxo's version of the myth as it relates to our theme, see note 106 below.

as the Mother of Three Giants. With this Óðinn took leave of Hel. As he did so, the Volva predicted the destruction of the world that was soon to come, the Ragnarök.

The next scene took place in the council chambers of the Æsir. After describing what he had learned in Hel about Baldr's dreams, Óðinn and the other gods formulated a plan to protect this beloved fellow-god, and, by extension, themselves as well, from the fate that had been prophesied. Their plan was a simple one. Frigg would require everything in the world to swear an oath of mercy to Baldr so that no evil would befall him. Fire and water, the stones and ores, trees and sicknesses, animals and birds, snakes and serpents—all these, and the vast multitude of other beings that make up a complete inventory of the world besides, were enjoined to promise that no harm would come to Baldr through them.

When this was accomplished, the gods were at ease once more and their fancy turned to mirth. To amuse themselves they had Baldr stand before them while they shot at him with arrows, struck him with swords, and pelted him with any number of things. True to the vows they had taken, none of the things that were hurled at the young god harmed him. And so it was that the gods paid homage to Baldr.

Looking on, the ambivalent Loki did not like what he saw. Disguising himself as an old woman he then asked Frigg if it was true that all things had taken the oath not to harm Baldr. Frigg confirmed that all things had sworn themselves harmless—all things, that is, except a tiny twig of mistletoe that grows west of Valhalla, which she had deemed too young to make an oath. Upon hearing of the mistletoe, the treacherous Loki immediately set out to fetch it. When he returned, he placed it in the hand of the blind Hod, and instructed him on how it should be thrown. Not realizing that it was mistletoe in his hand, Hod threw it as Loki had directed. Though Baldr had withstood the blows of everything else that had been thrown at him, the mistletoe immediately passed through him, killing him instantly.

The death of Baldr devastated the gods. They all lost the power of speech, and all were at a loss as to how to express their grief. Revenge would have been instantaneous had they not been standing on sanctified ground and thus been forbidden for the moment from seeking retribution. Frigg, hoping that Baldr could be ransomed from Hel, promised her love and favour to whoever would undertake such a journey. Hermod the Fleet, Óðinn's son, took up the challenge. Borrowing his father's horse he rode to Hel, while the remaining Æsir prepared for the funeral. Baldr was to be cremated aboard a burning ship. When his wife, Nanna, saw the ship upon which his body lay in state she died of grief and was placed alongside him. Meanwhile, Hermod reached Hel and told its matron of the weeping and lamenting of the gods. Baldr, he learned, would be allowed to return with him to live once more among the Æsir on the condition that everything living and dead in the world would join together in grief for him. The proviso to this, however, was that if there was even one exception to this universal grief, Baldr would have to remain in Hel.

Just as earlier a message had been sent throughout the world for everything to swear itself harmless against Baldr, now a message was sent out admonishing all things to grieve together in unison. Sharing in the loss of Baldr, a loss that spelled their own doom, the things of the world— the gods and mortals, animals and stones, rivers and trees, etc.—all joined together in a great tumult of lamentation. But here again there was one fateful exception. An old troll hag named Tokk refused to shed even a single tear for Baldr. As a result, Baldr could not be brought back from Hel. It was said by many that the troll hag, Tokk, was actually Loki in disguise. The conflagration that had been prophesied then took place. Loki, soon after being bound by the gods, broke loose from his bonds and the final battle, which claimed the lives of the gods, was waged. The destruction of the nine worlds, however, was followed shortly by a new creation. The world in which we now dwell came into being, populated by the progeny of a human couple who had been hidden away inside the World Tree.[3] Along with this new creation, the beautiful Baldr returned as well—hence his claim to be a dying and resurgent god.[4]

---

[3] Where Norse myth imagines a human couple surviving the Ragnarök or end of the gods, Jung theorizes about the anima and animus as mediators of the collective unconscious (the realm of the archetypes or former "gods"): "The collective unconscious as a whole presents itself to a man in feminine form. To a woman it appears in masculine form, and then I call it the *animus*." Jung, *CW* 18 § 187. With arguably the same phenomena in mind, Freud writes of the sexual figuration of the ego-ideal. For a discussion of Freud's notion of the sexual ideal in its relation to Jung's notion of the anima/animus, see my *The Dove in the Consulting Room: Hysteria and the Anima in Bollas and Jung* (Hove: Brunner-Routledge, 2003), pp. 129-130.

[4] Harald Hveberg, *Of Gods and Giants: Norse Mythology*, tr. P. S. Iversen (Oslo: Johan Grundt Tanum Forlag, 1969), pp. 62-68. My re-telling of Snorri Sturluson's version of the Baldr myth follows Hveberg's account. The dialogue is quoted from Hveberg's telling of this myth.

Part One: Baldr's Freud

Baldr's Death in Freud's Thought

Time in the soul is circular, a cycle of sacred moments, a ritual return to eternity, a compulsion to repeat. Torn from its living context in the religious practices of the ancient North, the Baldr myth reads as a narrative in time, a story with a beginning, middle, and end. Heard as an ever-recurring moment in sacred time, however, it has the character of a round. The Baldr who is killed by the gods despite their wish to spare him is always already the product of ceaseless repetitions of the same story. Similarly, the Baldr whom the gods cannot retrieve from Hel is perennially resurrected simply through the re-telling of his tale.

It is in this spirit that we shall be reading Freud. Like the ancient myths, Freud's theories also circle around a number of arcane themes in an effort to plumb the mysteries of the soul. Concepts are related to each other much as the gods are related to each other. Ideas concerning the mechanisms that govern the psychic life of contemporary men and women bear a filial resemblance to ideas concerning the emergence of life in the dim prehistory of the planet. At many junctures these theoretical ideas bear a strong resemblance to the events described in our myth. In Freud's writings, as we shall see, Baldr enacts himself with especial vividness in the interplay of theories and concepts having to do with the principles of constancy and pleasure, the origins of life, parricide, mourning, narcissism, the ego-ideal and civilization. Though each of these subjects differs from the others, they share a story together, a story, moreover, that is like the tale our Northern forebears told of that dying and resurgent god. To pull this story together, even as Snorri Sturluson pulled together his account of the Baldr myth from the ancient poetical sources available to him, we shall be examining the texts from Freud's writings which repeat the motifs of our Northern myth. As always, our intent in doing so is not to reduce or explain the one in terms of the other, but to throw into relief those aspects of the psyche which both apostrophize, each in their own way and for their own time.

As we survey Freud's books and papers in the light of the Baldr myth, there are specific titles that stand out as likely candidates for comparison. In his aspect as a god who stands apart from the other gods, Baldr brings to mind writings by Freud having to with the individual and his relations to society—*Group Psychology and the Analysis of the Ego* and *Civilization and its Discontents*. In his aspect as a god who dies and through his death occasions an almost universal grief, Baldr is suggestive of Freud's paper "Mourning and Melancholia" and his book *Totem and Taboo*. And in connection to his being a dying and the resurgent god who is so loved that the other gods do not wish to relinquish him, we are led to associate four further titles from Freud's oeuvre, "On Narcissism," *The Ego and the Id*, *Beyond the Pleasure Principle*, and the "Project for a Scientific Psychology." Though each of these works evokes itself in its entirety in the drama of our Norse myth, even as our Norse myth may be imagined to evoke itself in its entirety in them, we must here be content with brief sketches of the theoretical formulations appearing in these works that seem most redolent of the motifs of the Baldr myth.

The Principle of Constancy and the Pleasure Principle

> Through the forming of the ideal, what biology and the vicissitudes of the human species have created in the id and left behind in it is taken over by the ego and re-experienced in relation to itself as an individual. Owing to the way in which the ego ideal is formed, it has the most abundant links with the phylogenetic acquisition of each individual—his archaic heritage. What has belonged to the lowest part of the mental life of each of us is changed, through the formation of the ideal, into what is highest in the human mind by our scale of values.[5]

Read as an epiphany of Baldr, Freud's theories enact the story of that dying and resurgent god in the mechanistic account they provide of the origins and development of the ancestral soul. Though Freud does not use the term "ancestral soul" (preferring instead such terms as phylogeny, archaic vestiges, and collective mind), our use of it here underscores an important dimension of his psychological enterprise. An archaeologist of the psyche, Freud made a speculative descent into its depths, a descent that extended back past the generations of mankind to the earliest moments when life in its most basic forms emerged upon the earth. In addition to the Primal Father and his incest horde, which we

---

[5] Sigmund Freud, *The Ego and the Id*, ed., J. Strachey, tr. J. Riviere (New York: W. W. Norton, 1962), p. 26.

discussed in the previous chapter, Freud conceived of other, more distant
ancestors. Going farther back even than the primates, which Darwin held
to be the progenitors of human beings, Freud conceived of an amoeba-
like vesicle with a cortical layer that is susceptible to stimulation.[6] The
clay out of which this earliest of Adams came into being Freud believed
to be the chemical substance of the inorganic world. True to his
mechanistic bent, however, Freud portrayed the Divine Artificer not as
god, but as the forces known to the physics of his day.

The cornerstone of Freud's account of how the "phylogenetic
acquisitions" of the aeon-spanning ancestral soul come to be transformed
into our highest mental functions and cultural forms is the "principle
of constancy" or "tendency to stability." In this idea, which Freud
borrowed from Gustav T. Fechner, Baldr evokes himself in the simplest
and most elemental of terms. As adapted by Freud to the purposes of
psychoanalytic investigation, this psycho-physical principle states that
"the mental apparatus endeavors to keep the quantity of excitation present
in it as low as possible or at least to keep it constant."[7] In our myth we
find a similar motif. Though Baldr is the target of the projectiles hurled
at him by the gods, all of the projectiles, with the exception of the
mistletoe, have sworn themselves harmless against him. The image, here,
is one of stability; there is neither increase nor decrease. Suspended
between the prospect of death, as presaged in his dreams, and the prospect
of a continuance of life, as suggested by his apparent invulnerability to
harm, Baldr and his fellow gods ambivalently play both these ends of
existence against each other. This dynamic, as we shall see, recurs in many
of Freud's formulations.

Most immediately, we may be reminded by the mirth of the gods,
as they make sport with Baldr, of another facet of the constancy principle
Freud borrowed from Fechner. For Fechner, the psycho-physical tensions
that we experience as sensations of pain and pleasure are also a function
of this principle or tendency. Just as Baldr feels, not pain, but enjoyment
when struck with the objects which have promised Frigg they will not
harm him, so for Fechner "every psycho-physical motion rising above
the threshold of consciousness is attended by pleasure in proportion as,

---

[6] Sigmund Freud, *Beyond the Pleasure Principle*, tr. J. Strachey (New York: Norton,
1961), pp. 20-21, 42-43. See also, Freud's "On Narcissism: An Introduction," in *The
Freud Pelican Library*, vol. 11 (Harmondsworth: Penguin Books, 1991), pp. 67-68.
[7] Freud, *Beyond the Pleasure Principle*, p. 3.

beyond a certain limit, it approximates to complete stability, and is attended by unpleasure in proportion as, beyond a certain limit, it deviates from complete stability ...."[8]

Freud's notion of the pleasure principle is essentially an abbreviation of this formula of Fechner's. Predicating the principle of constancy to that of pleasure on the grounds that the constancy principle "was inferred from facts which forced [psychoanalysis] to adopt the pleasure principle,"[9] Freud, in effect, established a similar covenant within the economics of mental life as Frigg established in our myth. Like Frigg requiring all things to swear that they will not harm her son, the pleasure principle requires that all tensions discharge themselves as expeditiously as possible.

The fateful sprig of mistletoe to which Baldr falls prey in our myth enters this picture in Freud's recognition that the pleasure principle is not universally binding. Like Loki learning from Frigg about this plant that grew far away by the walls of Valhalla and which had made no promise to her, Freud recognized that there are mental processes which operate "*beyond* the pleasure principle."[10] "It must be pointed out," writes Freud, in a passage in which we can overhear Frigg's disclosure to Loki of the existence and whereabouts of the mistletoe,

> ... that strictly speaking it is incorrect to talk [as we did previously] of the dominance of the pleasure principle over the course of mental processes. If such a dominance existed, the immense majority of our mental processes would have to be accompanied by pleasure or to lead to pleasure, whereas universal experience completely contradicts any such conclusion. The most that can be said, therefore, is that there exists in the mind a strong *tendency* towards the pleasure principle, but that that tendency is opposed by certain other forces or circumstances, so that the final outcome cannot always be in harmony with the tendency towards pleasure. We may compare what Fechner ... remarks on a similar point: "Since however a tendency towards an aim does not imply that the aim is attained, and since in general the aim is attainable only by approximations ...."[11]

---

[8] Cited in Freud, *Beyond the Pleasure Principle*, p. 2.
[9] Freud, *Beyond the Pleasure Principle*, p. 3.
[10] Freud, *Beyond the Pleasure Principle*, p. 11.
[11] Freud, *Beyond the Pleasure Principle*, pp. 3-4.

Of Mistletoe, Repetition, and the Reality Principle

Among the forces or circumstances which operate in opposition to the pleasure principle's direct pursuit of its aims, two must be singled out as especially important in Freud's thought: the reality principle and the compulsion to repeat. The first of these, the reality principle, bears, at most, a superficial resemblance to the deadly stalk of mistletoe that brought doom to Baldr. Indeed, compared with the mistletoe that Freud hurled in his story of the dynamics of the psyche when he first proposed his concept of the compulsion to repeat, the reality principle is as benign as the projectiles that the gods fired at the impervious Baldr. This, however, is reason enough to discuss it briefly before turning our attention to that truly deadly force and most primordial of ancestors, the compulsion to repeat, or, as Freud also called it, the death-instinct.

While reality, with its characteristic harshness, continually challenges the pleasure principle by bringing to bear upon our lives events and circumstances incompatible with that principle's hedonic aims, the reality principle works in concert with the principle of pleasure by reckoning these events and circumstances into the latter's hedonic equation. Attuned to the possibilities of life that might interfere with the attainment of pleasure, the ego-instincts, serving the interests of self-preservation, carry "into effect the postponement of satisfaction, the abandonment of a number of possibilities of gaining satisfaction and the temporary toleration of unpleasure as a step on the long indirect road to pleasure."[12] It is through this interplay between the pleasure and reality principles that the gods of Freud's theory, the instincts,[13] become as "aim-inhibited" in their search for gratification as the Æsir were in theirs. Similarly, it is through this interplay of psychical principles that the Baldr-like ego, that "seat of anxiety,"[14] comes to marshall defenses against unpleasure.

But what about the mistletoe? Clearly, the reality principle, as we have just shown, bears a closer analogy to the Æsir and their sport of

---

[12] Freud, *Beyond the Pleasure Principle*, p. 4.

[13] Sigmund Freud, *New Introductory Lectures on Psychoanalysis*, in *The Freud Pelican Library*, vol. 2 (Harmondsworth: Penguin Books, 1988), p. 127: "...the theory of the instincts is so to say our mythology. Instincts are mythical entities, magnificent in their indefiniteness. In our work we cannot for a moment disregard them, yet we are never sure that we are seeing them clearly."

[14] Freud, *The Ego and the Id*, p. 47.

pelting Baldr than to this deadly twig. How then does the mistletoe evoke
itself in Freud's thought?

To find the mistletoe in Freud's writings we must, like Loki on his
trek to Valhalla, look further afield, to the outer reaches of Freud's
speculative thought, for as Freud himself admitted it was by speculating
wildly that he came upon his concept of the repetition compulsion and
the theory of its origins.[15]

The Compulsion to Repeat

Like the principle of constancy, the compulsion to repeat is subject
to a stabilizing tendency. This tendency to stability, however, is
more primitive than the one Fechner described in his analysis of
psycho-physical mechanisms or the one that Freud envisioned in his
related account of the pleasure principle. Heir to the inertia of lifeless
matter, the repetition compulsion is under the sway of the great,
great, infinitely great grandfather of these later principles and
processes. Driven by that most ancestral of all urges, the urge to
return to the stability of the inorganic world, the compulsion to
repeat runs roughshod over the equilibriums in which the sentient
organs that Fechner studied and the mental apparatus that Freud
described seek to operate, leaving pain, destruction, and death in its
wake. It is these fateful effects—pain, destruction, and death—that
this havoc-wreaking force, the compulsion to repeat, keeps constant
in our lives.

Among the clinical manifestations of the repetition compulsion,
Freud included the whole range of destructive behaviours that cannot
be accounted for exclusively within the economics of the pleasure and
reality principles. The Baldr-like trauma dream is one example;[16] the
negative therapeutic reaction another.[17] Also important are those recurrent
tragedies of life which afflict even our most blameless patients. Having
done nothing in any active way to arrange their own demise, these
patients seem to be obliged by the uncanny course of the events befalling

---

[15] As Freud writes in the preamble to his discussion of the repetition compulsion:
"What follows is speculation, often far-fetched speculation, which the reader will
consider or dismiss according to his individual predilection." *Beyond the Pleasure
Principle*, p. 18.

[16] Freud, *Beyond the Pleasure Principle*, p. 26.

[17] Freud, *The Ego and the Id*, pp. 39-40.

them to suffer in oddly tragic ways.[18] Marching to the beat of a psychic factor that is clearly beyond the pleasure principle (and beyond the reality principle, too, for that matter), these patients appear to be the victims of a daemonic power of fate.[19] Seconding Heraclitus, who wrote that "a man's character is his fate,"[20] Freud saw in these compulsively repetitive enactments of the way things happen the workings of deeply unconscious character resistances which are not personal, but instinctual, in origin.

With our Northern myth in mind, let us now examine several passages from Freud's writings in which he speculates about the origins of this death-seeking compulsion which, like the mistletoe, was never made to swear itself harmless against us. (As we do so it will be important to bear in mind that what Freud conceives of as a death-instinct, more archaic myths represent as an order of existence that is composed of the dead, i.e., the underworld, or Hel, of the ancestors.)

In the first of these quotations, Freud identifies the compulsion to repeat as a natural tendency acting through the instincts. Framing his reflections with the question, "But how is the predicate of being 'instinctual' related to the compulsion to repeat?" he writes:

> ... [W]e cannot escape a suspicion that we may have come upon the track of a universal attribute of instincts and perhaps of organic life in general which has not hitherto been clearly recognized. ... *It seems, then, that an instinct is an urge inherent in organic life to restore an earlier state of things* which the living entity has been obliged to abandon under the pressure of external disturbing forces; that is, it is a kind of organic elasticity, or, to put it another way, the expression of the inertia inherent in organic life.[21]

---

[18] Freud, *Beyond the Pleasure Principle*, p. 16: "This 'perpetual recurrence of the same thing' causes us no astonishment when it relates to *active* behaviour on the part of the person concerned and when we can discern in him an essential character-trait which always remains the same and which is compelled to find expression in a repetition of the same experiences. We are much more impressed by cases where the subject appears to have a *passive* experience, over which he has no influence, but in which he meets with a repetition of the same fatality. There is the case, for instance, of the woman who married three successive husbands each of whom fell ill soon afterwards and had to be nursed by her on their death-beds."

[19] Freud, *Beyond the Pleasure Principle*, p. 29: "The manifestations of a compulsion to repeat ... exhibit to a high degree an instinctual character and, when they act in opposition to the pleasure principle, give the appearance of some 'daemonic' force at work."

[20] Heraclitus, fragment 121.

[21] Freud, *Beyond the Pleasure Principle*, p. 30.

Rider bound for Hel conveys Freud's notion of the death-instinct

Read alongside our Norse myth, as a variation of its vision of the way things happen, it is precisely here, in his characterization of instinct as "an urge inherent in organic life to restore an earlier state of things" that Freud lets the death-dealing mistletoe fly. Though seemingly innocuous, like the little plant that Frigg deemed too trifling to be required to swear itself harmless, our instincts, for Freud, are subject to a compulsion to replicate or return to the stability of the inorganic world, the world out of which all life must once have originated. The inorganic world, of course, is an inanimate world and, so, to return to it is to return to death. As Freud puts it, "we shall be compelled to say that *'the aim of all life is death'* and, looking backwards, that *'inanimate things existed before living ones.'"*[22]

Progressing Deathward to No Death

Acting against this drive to death, according to Freud, is "the pressure of external disturbing forces," which, like the projectiles that the Æsir throw at Baldr, oblige the instincts and their organic substrate to abandon, or better said, postpone their return to the inert stabilities of inanimate matter. The picture here is that of a mechanistic dialectic. On the one hand, there is something comparable to the principle of constancy operative in the chemical processes which are at play in the inorganic world. On the other hand, there are disturbing factors that interfere with these processes in such a way that life negentropically gets a toehold.[23]

Expressed in the language of our myth, it is not just that Baldr's death is postponed because of the promise of the world's objects not to harm him. More deeply considered, *his life and spirit are the product of this same process.* A dying and resurgent god, Baldr lives by means of dying. Subject to the fatal mistletoe from the very beginning of life, even as all things can be said to be born dying, he lives that deferral of death we have learned to call life on account of the perturbing influence of the objects thrown

---

[22] Freud, *Beyond the Pleasure Principle*, p. 32.

[23] Negentropy is a concept introduced into evolutionary theory by the physicist Erwin Schrödinger about twenty years after Freud wrote *Beyond the Pleasure Principle*. As Arthur Koestler writes, "'Negative entropy' (or 'negentropy') is ... a somewhat perverse way of referring to the power of living organisms to 'build up' instead of running down, to create complex structures out of simpler elements, integrated patterns out of shapelessness, order out of disorder. The same irrepressible building-up tendency is manifested in the progress of evolution, the emergence of new levels of complexity in the organismic hierarchy and new methods of functional coordination, resulting in greater independence from, and mastery of, the environment." Arthur Koestler, *Janus: A Summing Up* (London: Hutchinson, 1978), p. 223.

at him by the Æsir. These objects, operating within the precincts of the
pleasure and reality principles, create a dialectic which forestalls the
repetition compulsion, at least until Loki hands the mistletoe to the blind
Hod. Reading the myth as a round, it is easy to imagine that the objects
which now fall harmlessly upon Baldr were as fatal as the mistletoe during
previous incarnations at earlier levels of evolution and culture. As Freud
puts it in a key passage:

> The attributes of life were at some time evoked in inanimate
> matter by the action of a force of whose nature we can form
> no conception. It may perhaps have been a process similar
> in type to that which later caused the development of
> consciousness in a particular stratum of living matter. The
> tension which then arose in what had hitherto been an
> inanimate substance endeavoured to cancel itself out. In this
> way the first instinct came into being: the instinct to return
> to the inanimate state. It was still an easy matter at that time
> for a living substance to die; the course of its life was
> probably only a brief one, whose direction was determined
> by the chemical structure of the young life. For a long time,
> perhaps, living substance was thus being constantly created
> afresh and easily dying, till decisive external influences altered
> in such a way as to oblige the still surviving substance to
> diverge ever more widely from its original course of life and
> to make every more complicated *détours* before reaching its
> aim of death. These circuitous paths to death, faithfully kept
> to by the conservative instincts, would thus present us to-
> day with the picture of the phenomena of life. If we firmly
> maintain the exclusively conservative nature of instincts, we
> cannot arrive at any other notions as to the origin and aim
> of life.[24]

From an archetypal point of view, this passage of Freud's can be
characterized as a creation myth. More particularly, it can be seen as a
recurrence in conceptual language of the familiar motif of the dying and
resurgent god, the so-called son-lover of the Great Mother. Comparison
with the myth of Baldr bears this out even in detail. The figures we have
been discussing from our myth are easily recognizable in this passage.
Baldr, as we have already seen, bears witness to himself in phrases such as

---

[24] Freud, *Beyond the Pleasure Principle*, pp. 32-33.

"the attributes of life [which] were at some time evoked," "the young life," and the "living substance [which] was thus being constantly created afresh and easily dying." The projectile-hurling Æsir, likewise, evoke themselves in the reference to "decisive external influences." And the deadly mistletoe can be imaginatively conceived to enact itself in Freud's references to the "instinct to return to the inanimate state" and "conservative instincts," even as in the previously quoted passage we recognized it in Freud's definition of instinct as *an urge inherent in organic life to restore an earlier state of things.*"

Freud Consults the Volva

Other figures from our myth also reside in Freud's text. Just as the resurgent Baldr, the projectile-hurling Æsir, the protective Frigg, and the mistletoe-bearing Loki can be said to enact themselves in Freud's negentropic theory of the potentiating effect death has upon life, so Óðinn and Hermod can be said to enact their respective journeys to Hel on Baldr's behalf in Freud's theory of the "complicated detours" and "circuitous paths" followed by the living substance before reaching its final aim, the inanimate condition of death and stasis.

Hearing tell of the portentous nature of Baldr's dreams, Óðinn, as we recounted above, mounted his steed Sleipnir and rode to Hel to consult the Volva concerning his son's fate. Doubtless, the natural association that exists between dreams and death may be regarded as an important factor mobilizing Óðinn to set out on that "circuitous path" to death (Hel) which Freud discusses in more abstract terms in *Beyond the Pleasure Principle.* Simply put, since dreams come from the realm of death, it is to that realm that Óðinn must go to discern their meaning.[25]

There are, however, still other factors at play in Óðinn's journey to Hel, intrinsic ones which pertain to the character of that god. In the myth and religion of the North, Óðinn is a necromancer. As such he is able to glean prophetic knowledge from the skulls of the dead. Like Thanatos (both the Thanatos of the Greeks and the Thanatos referenced by Freud's followers when speaking of Freud's theory of the death-instinct), Óðinn is also a Lord of the Dead. In Valhalla, the old stories inform us, he holds

---

[25] For a thorough discussion on the relationship of dreams to death, that at the same time elucidates the mythological background of Freud's theory in relation to the Greek mythologem of the underworld, see James Hillman, *The Dream and the Underworld* (New York: Harper & Row, 1979), pp. 7-67.

nightly feasts for a host of warriors who have been killed in battle. As part of the eternal round, these feasting warriors take to the battlefield again each day, there to die once more in a fresh battle. "For a long time," writes Freud with respect to the similar drama played out in the chemical processes of matter, "… living substance was thus being constantly created afresh and easily dying …" (as quoted above).

Óðinn's horse, Sleipnir, also has associations with death. Most telling in this regard is the resemblance of its eight legs to the eight legs of a group of four pallbearers. From the asymmetrical viewpoint of the mythologizing psyche, a coffin and the party carrying it manifest the eight-legged horse of death, the steed of Óðinn, Sleipnir. In the mythic account of Baldr's death this apperceptive link is evident. At precisely the same time as the pallbearers cart the coffin of the dead Baldr away to his death-ship for cremation, Hermod rides Sleipnir to Hel in the hope of ransoming his beloved brother from death.

Negentropic Mourning

In "Mourning and Melancholia," Freud tells a story of loss and grief that is similar to our Northern myth. Like Óðinn, Frigg, and the other Æsir, the bereaved, according to Freud, are subject in their grief to immense resistances when faced with the task of relinquishing their deceased loved ones. These resistances, as we shall discuss in greater detail below, are redolent of the negentropic process of development we have been describing in our account of Freud's mechanistic vision of the origins of living matter, the instincts, and the mental apparatus. Though familiar to us on the level of our own personal experience, they have also an impersonal prehistory or archaic resonance—life's first emergence out of the inorganic world being a function of what has more recently been characterized as a failure or inability to mourn. Just as the Æsir in our myth (and we, too, in the throes of bereavement) are reluctant to be parted from deceased loved ones, so that force which operates beyond the pleasure principle to restore an earlier state of things can be said to enact a rudimentary form of the same resistive process.

While simultaneously bearing in mind the events of our Northern myth and our previous discussion of how these events recur in Freud's thought, let us now examine a passage in which Freud describes the dynamics of mourning.

The testing of reality, having shown that the loved object no longer exists, requires forthwith that all the libido shall be withdrawn from its attachments to this object. Against this demand a struggle of course arises—it may be universally observed that man never willingly abandons a libido-position, not even when a substitute is already beckoning to him. This struggle can be so intense that a turning away from reality ensues, the object being clung to through the medium of a hallucinatory wish-psychosis. The normal outcome is that deference for reality gains the day. Nevertheless its behest cannot be at once obeyed. The task is now carried through bit by bit, under great expense of time and cathectic energy, while all the time the existence of the lost object is continued in the mind. Each single one of the memories and hopes which bound the libido to the object is brought up and hyper-cathected, and the detachment of the libido from it accomplished. Why this process of carrying out the behest of reality bit by bit, which is in the nature of a compromise, should be so extraordinarily painful is not at all easy to explain in terms of mental economics. It is worth noting that this pain seems natural to us. The fact is, however, that when the work of mourning is completed the ego becomes free and uninhibited again.[26]

The resonances between Freud's account of the work of mourning and the myth of Baldr are many. Echoes not only of Óðinn and Hermod's journey to Hel, but also of the Æsir pelting the doomed Baldr can be overheard in Freud's reference to the tendency to turn away from the reality of loss and cling to the dead through the medium of "a hallucinatory wish-psychosis." Just as the objects that the Æsir throw at Baldr both swear themselves harmless against him and promise to join together in grief for him, so Freud writes of the "bit by bit" process by which "each single one of the memories and hopes which bound the libido to the object is brought up and hyper-cathected" in order that the "detachment of libido from it may be accomplished."

---

[26] Sigmund Freud, "Mourning and Melancholia," in *Collected Papers*, vol. IV: 152-170, tr. J. Riviere (London: The Hogarth Press & The Institute of Psycho-Analysis, 1950), p. 154. (All subsequent references to the *Collected Papers*—hereafter *CP*—will be by volume and page number.)

In the last sentence of this quotation, Freud speaks of the ego becoming free and uninhibited again with the completion of the work of mourning. While this statement accurately describes the fact that people more or less do resolve their losses and, after a period of mourning, form new attachments, it does not deal with the opposite case, in which the object is not relinquished and the work of mourning is not completed in this sense. For an account of this process, which, though clinically troubling, is surprisingly rich in negentropic contributions when viewed in phylogenetic perspective, we turn now to a passage from *The Ego and the Id*. While keeping our myth in mind, it is also important for our discussion to broaden the meaning of the term "ego" by noting that for Freud the ego is not only an institution in the human mind, but an aspect of simpler life forms as well, insofar as a dermis or surface-boundary is produced in them as "the inevitable expression of the influence of the external world."[27]

> When it happens that a person [or simpler life form, as just noted—G. M] has to give up a sexual object, there quite often ensues an alteration of his ego which can only be described as a setting up of the object inside the ego ...; the exact nature of this substitution is as yet unknown to us. It may be that by this introjection ... the ego makes it easier for the object to be given up, or renders that process possible. It may be that this identification is the sole condition under which the id can give up its objects. At any rate the process, especially in the early phases of development, is a very frequent one, and it makes it possible to suppose that the character of the ego is a precipitate of abandoned object-cathexes and that it contains the history of those object-choices.[28]

Enacting the Æsir's reluctance to relinquish Baldr in his account of man's resistance to giving up a loved object, Freud provides a mythical account of his own of the mechanism by which the ancestral soul is generated. Like the Æsir in their attempt to forestall Baldr's passing away

---

[27] Freud, *The Ego and the Id*, p. 28: "The differentiation between the ego and the id must be attributed not only to primitive man but even to much simpler organisms, for it is the inevitable expression of the influence of the external world." Freud here refers to the outer dermis of organisms, to the bark of trees, the rind of fruits and vegetables, and the shells of mollusks, etc.

[28] Freud, *The Ego and the Id*, p. 19.

by such means as journeys to Hel and universal lamentation, lost objects, for Freud, are set up inside the renunciative, hypercathected ego through the twin processes of identification and introjection. In this way the urge to restore an earlier state of things is satisfied at a negentropically higher level of organization. The mourning process, evidently, is not only about letting go of the dead—though of course they are relinquished in a physical sense. Additionally, it is about retaining them on higher and higher levels of complexity. Ironically, when seen in vast phylogenetic perspective, it is the failures of the mourning process that provide descendents of the dead with the negative capability (Keats) to carry out the part of its work that can be completed during the course of their own particular lives.

In the Norse account of the way these things happen, the troll hag Tokk will not grieve for the dead Baldr, with the result that the campaign to restore him to life fails. In Freud's account, the life-creating, psyche-constituting negentropic process to which we are heir is the result of our forebears having identified themselves with lost loved ones that they, too, could not fully relinquish or grieve. Though the ego, that "inevitable expression of the influence of the external world," has reached its most advanced flowering in the values and ideals we now share together as civilized human beings, these characterological acquisitions are, as Freud writes in the quotation above, "a precipitate of abandoned object-cathexis ... that ... contains the history of those object-choices."

Another passage from *The Ego and the Id* may be cited at this juncture for the vivid picture it presents of how the processes we have been discussing work together to constitute what I, with Jung's notion of the collective unconscious in mind, am calling the ancestral soul:

> ... [N]o external vicissitudes can be experienced or undergone by the id, except by way of the ego .... The experiences of the ego seem at first to be lost for inheritance; but, when they have been repeated often enough and with sufficient strength in many individuals in successive generations, they transform themselves, so to say, into experiences of the id, the impressions of which are preserved by heredity. Thus in the id, which is capable of being inherited, are harboured residues of the existences of countless egos; and, when the ego forms its super-ego [read ego-ideal—G. M.] out of the id, it

may perhaps only be reviving shapes of former egos and
be bringing them to resurrection.[29]

In visualizing that imaginal process which Freud described as "a
setting up of the [lost or relinquished] object inside the ego,"[30] it is
important to recognize that the ego to which Freud refers is not the
Jungian ego. In Jung's definition, the ego is simply the centre of
consciousness. For Freud, on the other hand, the ego, as an expression
of the circuitous, negentropic process of dying into life, has an
unconscious aspect as well. This unconscious aspect, which Freud called
the "third unconscious,"[31] is the dead zone in which the lost objects are
set up. The conscious part of the ego resides, as it were, behind these
identifications. They are not in it; on the contrary, it is in them. The
dead, that is to say, do not live on in the mind. The mind carries on in
the dead.[32]

Freud communicates his vision of the negentropic origins of the
conscious part of the ego by asking us to picture a "living vesicle with
[a] receptive cortical layer" suspended like Baldr "in the middle of an
external world charged with the most powerful energies." "This little
fragment," he continues,

> ... would be killed by the stimulation emanating from these
> if it were not provided with a protective shield against
> stimuli. It acquires the shield in this way: its outermost
> surface ceases to have the structure proper to living matter,
> becomes to some degree inorganic and thenceforward
> functions as a special envelope or membrane resistant to
> stimuli. In consequence, the energies of the external world
> are able to pass into the next underlying layers, which have
> remained living, with only a fragment of their original
> intensity; and these layers can devote themselves, behind the
> protective shield, to the reception of the amounts of stimulus

---

[29] Freud, *The Ego and the Id*, p. 28.
[30] Freud, *The Ego and the Id*, p. 19.
[31] Freud, *The Ego and the Id*, pp. 7-8. With the notion of a "third Ucs.," Freud
postulates the existence of an unconscious that is more like the Jungian unconscious
in that it does not correspond to the repressed but to a psychical substrate which has
never been conscious. In contrast to Jung, however, Freud locates this unconscious in
the ego. Known to us through character resistances, it is continuous with the "crust,"
"cortical layer," or dead zone which has been created by the impact of the external world.
[32] Cf. my "The After-Life of the Image: On Jung and Mourning," *Spring 71: A
Journal of Archetype and Culture* (New Orleans: Spring Journal, 2004), pp. 89-111.

which have been allowed through it. By its death, the outer layer has saved all the deeper ones from a similar fate—unless, that is to say, stimuli reach it [as the mistletoe reached Baldr—G. M.] which are so strong that they break through the protective shield. *Protection against* stimuli is an almost more important function for the living organism than *reception of* stimuli. ... The main purpose of the *reception* of stimuli is to discover the direction and nature of the external stimuli; and for that it is enough to take small specimens of the external world, to sample it in small quantities.[33]

Reading this passage we are at once reminded of Freud's speculative account of the origins of life and of our earlier exploration of how Freud's views on this subject enact the myth of Baldr's death. Our discussion at that juncture, it will be recalled, centred around a quotation from *Beyond the Pleasure Principle* in which Freud states that while we can form no conception of the force that first caused the attributes of life to appear in inanimate matter, "it may have been a process similar in type to that which later caused the development of consciousness in a particular stratum of living matter."[34] In the passage to which our attention is now directed, Freud picks up on this suggestion. Heir to the life-creating tension that was prevented from cancelling itself out by the impingement of external disturbing forces (even as Baldr lived by virtue of what the Æsir hurled at him), the living fragment which is suspended amidst the powerful energies of the world negentropically continues the battle of Eros against Thanatos, life against death. Shielded from the overwhelming intensities of stimuli reaching it from without by that part of itself which has already been overwhelmed and killed, the living fragment brings the Baldr-like process of dying into life to a higher level by developing sentient awareness. On the one hand, we may imagine with Freud a physical process: "... as a result of the ceaseless impact of external stimuli on the surface of the vesicle, its substance to a certain depth may have been permanently modified, so that excitatory processes run a different course in it from what they run in the deeper layers. A crust would thus be formed which would at last have been so thoroughly 'baked through' by stimulation that it would present the most favourable possible conditions

---

[33] Freud, *Beyond the Pleasure Principle*, p. 21.
[34] Freud, *Beyond the Pleasure Principle*, pp. 32-33.

for the reception of stimuli and become incapable of further modification."[35] On the other hand, we may imagine, again with Freud, that this same process has a psychological aspect based in the tendency of the negentropically evolving life-substance to identify with and introject the objects of its environment and aspects of itself which it is resistant to relinquishing. "[Unwilling to] abandon a libido position, ... even when a substitute is already beckoning,"[36] the mental apparatus, following in the ancestral footsteps of the processes that have transpired from time immemorial in the natural history of the living substance, takes on the character of the object to which it had been attached. "Thus," writes Freud, "the shadow of the [lost] object fell upon the ego, so that the latter could henceforth be criticized by a special mental faculty like an object, like the forsaken object."[37]

The Ego-Ideal

Earlier we quoted a text from Freud's writings in which he said that "what biology and the vicissitudes of the human species have created in the id and left behind in it is taken over by the ego and re-experienced in relation to itself as an individual."[38] The referent in this quotation, it will be recalled, was the ego-ideal, that highest of mental structures which, nevertheless, "has the most abundant links with the phylogenetic acquisitions of each individual—his archaic heritage." At this juncture, having discussed the manner in which the dying and resurgent Baldr enacts himself in Freud's neo-vitalist vision of the most primordial moments and phases of the archaic heritage to which the ego and its ideal are heir, we may now bring this entire negentropic, evolutionary process to bear upon these higher forms of the mind and culture.

In the tale of Baldr's death and attempted resurrection, the objects hurled at the young god miraculously cause him no harm. Through the use of the technical terms "ego" and "ego-ideal," Freud also described a state in which the "slings and arrows of outrageous fortune" strike lightly, causing little damage. Prior to the differentiations which later bear upon them, infants and small children cavort like the unscathed Baldr in a world with which they are one. Protected by parental love, even as Baldr

[35] Freud, *Beyond the Pleasure Principle,* p. 20.
[36] Freud, "Mourning and Melancholia," p. 154.
[37] Freud, "Mourning and Melancholia," p. 159.
[38] Freud, *The Ego and the Id,* p. 26.

was protected by Frigg, their narcissism enjoys a brief immunity from the impingements that the environment hurls their way. As in our Northern myth, however, this state of original, or, as Freud also calls it, primary narcissism is not completely impervious to the impingements of fate.[39] Just as Loki places the deadly sprig of mistletoe into the hand of the blind Hod, so life has a way of dealing a fatal blow to the narcissistic perfection of those early days when, as Freud put it, the child is his own ideal. Not forever will the world obey the protective edicts of the family, swear itself harmless, and adapt to the child as to a beautiful young god. Indeed, sooner or later, even the parents themselves will hurl the mistletoe, if only in the form of increasing expectations.[40]

It is precisely here, in the mortal blows which life deals to our narcissism, that Freud locates the ontogenetic origins of the ego. Like Baldr, impervious to the projectiles fired upon him by the gods, the ego, for Freud, develops out of an undifferentiated state in which the impulsions of instinct are at one with their satiating object even as the child is at one with its mother. This feeling of inchoate oneness, or as Freud calls it, primary narcissism, corresponds to the "oceanic feeling" which the poet Romain Rolland, anticipating our present discussion of the divine background of Freud's theories, claimed to be the true referent of religious sentiments. In Rolland's view, as Freud recounts it in the first

---

[39] Sigmund Freud, *An Outline of Psychoanalysis*, tr. J. Strachey (New York: W. W. Norton, 1963), p. 23. Writing with reference to what he calls "absolute, primary *narcissism*," Freud states that this condition "continues until the ego begins to cathect the presentations [i.e., images] of objects with libido—to change narcissistic libido into *object libido*." These lines are transparent to the myth of Baldr, in particular to the scene of the myth having to do with the god's being pelted with objects. Baldr's imperviousness to the objects, his indifference to them, reflects what Freud would call the state prior to the cathecting of objects, i.e., the condition of primary narcissism. By the same token, this scene from the myth could also be compared to Freud's account of the subsequent, cathecting stage, in which objects are invested with interest and the narcissistic libido is changed into object libido. The mistletoe enters Freud's text a few lines later when he writes about the main quantity of libido coming to be directed onto one particular object which then, as a love object, has the quality of an ego.

[40] When the world is not a good-enough world, when, that is to say, the slings and arrows of fate are more than Frigg can mediate, the gap between what Freud called the ego and the ego-ideal becomes greater such that the latter becomes more burdensome and persecutory. The deadly sprig of mistletoe, according to this account, is anything that happens to the evolving life form at any stage of development which is in excess of the equilibriums in which that life form optimally exists. Winnicott speaks of failures of the facilitating environment and of impingements on the transitional space which curtail the play or spontaneous gesture of the child. It is in these terms that Baldr enacts himself in the thought of this more recent psychoanalytic theorist. See Donald W. Winnicott, *The Maturational Process and the Facilitating Environment* (New York: International Universities Press, 1965).

pages of *Civilization and its Discontents*, there exists "a feeling of an indissoluble bond, of being one with the external world as a whole."[41] In the terms of our myth, this oneness with the external world which the mother mediates corresponds to Baldr's invulnerability with respect to the objects that are thrown at him by the Æsir. Just as the Norse myth depicts Baldr as being at one with the world in which all things have sworn themselves harmless at the behest of Frigg, so psychological theory conceives of the child as experiencing a period of optimal rapport with the mother until her attunement to him shifts.

Regaining Lost Worlds on New Levels

While exploring the manner in which Baldr enacts himself in these notions of Freud's, let us also bear in mind our earlier discussion of how he enacts himself in Freud's vision of primordial processes. It will be recalled that Freud saw a parallel between the development of life out of inorganic matter and the development of consciousness in a particular stratum of living matter. In much the same way, the development of the ego during the period in which the child luxuriates in the protective embrace of its mother may be regarded as a repetition, at a much higher level of development, of this same process. Indeed, just as in our earlier account of how the disturbing external influences caused the characteristics of life to develop out of what had hitherto been inorganic matter, so the child's ego develops by virtue of the challenge posed by the painful sensations which impinge upon the blissful state of primary narcissism which exists briefly between the child and its mother. Though the child, so long as he enjoys the protection afforded him by maternal love, lives, like Baldr protected by Frigg, in a world of objects which have sworn themselves harmless against him, he gradually learns to differentiate himself as a subject from the external world (i.e., the mother) in response to various contingencies. Subject to the "slings and arrows of outrageous fortune," some of which are mediated by the father,[42] the

---

[41] Sigmund Freud, *Civilization and its Discontents*, in *The Freud Pelican Library*, vol. 12: pp. 251-340 (Harmondsworth: Penguin Books, 1985), p. 252.

[42] The father of the Oedipal period is like the mistletoe of our myth, not because he mediates the reality principle, but because the child's inner representation of him during this time is a function of phylogenetic schemata which are grounded in the compulsion to repeat. For Freud, the child's relationship to the father is heir to the violence with which the primal father dominated his horde in prehistoric times. And

pleasure ego, like Baldr, is eventually slain and a reality ego resurrected in its stead. As Freud expresses this in a passage that is especially rich with motifs of the Baldr myth,

> ... disengagement of the ego from the general mass of sensations—that is, ... recognition of an 'outside,' and external world—is provided by the frequent, manifold and unavoidable sensations of pain and unpleasure the removal and avoidance of which is enjoined by the pleasure principle, in the exercise of its unrestricted domination. A tendency arises to separate from the ego everything that can become a source of such unpleasure, to throw it outside and to create a pure pleasure-ego which is confronted by a strange and threatening 'outside.' The boundaries of this primitive pleasure-ego cannot escape rectification through experience. Some of the things that one is unwilling to give up, because they give pleasure, are nevertheless not ego but object; and some sufferings that one seeks to expel turn out to be inseparable from the ego in virtue of their internal origin. One comes to learn a procedure by which, through a deliberate direction of one's sensory activities and through suitable muscular action, one can differentiate between what is internal—what belongs to the ego—and what is external—what emanates from the outer world. In this way one makes the first step towards the introduction of the reality principle which is to dominate future development. ... In this way, ... the ego detaches itself from the external world. Or, to put it more correctly, originally the ego includes everything, later it separates off an external world from itself. Our present ego-feeling is, therefore, only a shrunken residue of a much more inclusive—indeed, an all-embracing—feeling which corresponded to a more intimate bond between the ego and the world about it.[43]

But what happens to the narcissistic libido which the ego has had to forfeit in order to develop into a distinct entity? Like the dying and resurgent Baldr, the narcissistic cathexis of libido which has had to be forfeited in order for the ego to differentiate itself no sooner passes away

---

this, in turn, is heir to a dialectic between the inertia of inanimate matter and the play of external forces from which life emerged.

[43] Freud, *Civilization and its Discontents*, pp. 254-255.

than it resurrects itself in the form of an ideal through the aforementioned processes of identification and introjection. Past tense becomes future tense. Super-ego replaces Id. All that we have lost—both ontogenetically and phylogenetically—we feel ourselves exhorted to have again in some form. In the words of the poet, the child becomes the father of the man.[44]

This dynamic, whereby what is lost or renounced is not fully relinquished, but on the contrary, retained in the form of a part of the mental apparatus which has re-made itself in its image and likeness, is characteristic of the nature of libido. Like Óðinn, Frigg, and the other Æsir in their reluctance to relinquish the dead Baldr, "Man," as we have already heard from Freud, is "incapable of giving up a gratification he has once enjoyed." It is as a response to this incapacity to give up, or better said, this capacity to retain, that the ego-ideal comes into being.

Two quotes from Freud are particularly relevant here. The first of these, from his paper "On Narcissism," shows how the ego-ideal (heir to the negentropic process we have been describing) develops out of the ego-constituting renunciation of primary narcissism. The second quotation, taken from *Group Psychology and the Analysis of the Ego*, summarizes the diverse functions of the ego-ideal. As with all the texts we have cited, these may also be read with our myth in mind. (I suggest reading "Hel" for "repression," "Baldr's dreams" for "the censorship of dream," "the projectiles of the gods" for "influences of the environment," and so on.)

> The development of the ego consists in a departure from the primary narcissism and results in a vigorous attempt to recover it. This departure is brought about by means of the displacement of libido to an ego-ideal imposed from without, while gratification is derived from the attainment of this ideal.[45]

> ... [W]e have been driven to the hypothesis that some such agency develops in our ego which may cut itself off from the rest of the ego and come into conflict with it. We have called it the "ego-ideal," and by way of functions we have ascribed to it self-observation, the moral conscience, the censorship of dreams, and the chief influence in repression. We have said that it is heir to the original narcissism in which the childish ego enjoyed self-sufficiency; it gradually gathers up from the

---

[44] William Wordsworth, "Ode: Intimations of Immortality From Recollections of Early Childhood," 1st line of epigraph.
[45] Sigmund Freud, "On Narcissism: an Introduction," *CP* IV, p. 57.

influences of the environment the demands which that environment makes upon the ego and which the ego cannot always rise to; so that a man, when he cannot be satisfied with his ego itself, may nevertheless be able to find satisfaction in the ego ideal which has been differentiated out of the ego. In delusions of observation, as we have further shown, the disintegration of this agency has become patent, and has thus revealed its origin in the influence of superior powers, and above all of parents. But we have not forgotten to add that the amount of distance between this ego ideal and the real ego is very variable from one individual to another, and that with many people this differentiation within the ego does not go further than with children.[46]

While the distance between the ego and the ego-ideal may vary from individual to individual such that in some it goes no further than in children, the gap between the individual and what Freud called the cultural super-ego is immense. In *Civilization and its Discontents* Freud presents a picture of just how immense, and persecutory of the individual and his happiness, this gap in fact is. The instinctual renunciations which mankind has had to make in order to live together as a group become a "dynamic fount of conscience," demanding, in their turn, still further renunciation.[47] Civilized life is a life lived in the midst of the ghostly values through which we retain, in the form of binding expectations upon ourselves and our future, all that we and our forefathers, right back to the simple vesicle itself, have had to renounce or repress due to external traumatic factors and the obsessive imperatives of earlier ideals.[48] Little wonder that the individual stands in something of the same relationship to those with whom he shares common ideals as Freud's Baldr-like vesicle

---

[46] Sigmund Freud, "Group Psychology and the Analysis of the Ego," in *The Freud Pelican Library*, vol. 12: pp. 93-178 (Harmondsworth: Penguin Books, 1985), pp. 139-140.

[47] Freud, *Civilization and its Discontents*, p 321: "Every renunciation of instinct now becomes a dynamic source of conscience and every fresh renunciation increases the latter's severity and intolerance."

[48] By "earlier ideals" I mean, more precisely, the regularities of order that negentropically arise in the evolutionary/developmental process making the route to death more and more circuitous. Freud seems to have just this picture in mind when he writes that "Order is a kind of compulsion to repeat which, when a regulation has been laid down once and for all, decides when, where and how a thing shall be done, so that in every similar circumstance one is spared hesitation and indecision" (*Civilization and its Discontents*, p. 282). This account of order maps something of the same territory as does the notion of an archetypal pattern of behavior in Jung's thought.

stands with respect to the stimuli that the environment, like the projectile-hurling Æsir, directs its way.

The more the individual sets himself apart from the group as an individual, the more circuitous a detour he creates for the libido bequeathed to him by his forebears, and the more discontent and guilt he must tolerate. Having shed the protection provided by group affiliation, however, the individual may easily fall prey to the unmediated impact of the cultural values that bear in upon him. The rare epochal individual, such as Freud's *Egyptian* Moses,[49] on the other hand, may himself be the mistletoe that brings the Ragnarök of destruction and renewal upon the world of our cultural values, insofar as the tension he holds and the ethic he manifests surpass the moral level of the collective from which he has emerged.

Besides such epochal figures, there is another source of optimism and hope. Mitigating the grimly deterministic character of his mechanistic vision of the ancestral soul, Freud, almost in retrospect, introduced the notion of "an internal impulse towards 'progress' and towards higher development!"[50] Like Baldr returning in the new creation after the destruction of the gods, Eros, for Freud, is a positive instinctual force which is conservative even to a greater degree than the death-instinct in that it repeats again and again the beginning process of development wherein the first animate tensions arose.[51] By forming new unions along sexual lines, Eros continually introduces "fresh tensions" into the picture.[52] With his recognition of Eros as a force that is not simply reducible to his former concept of a pleasure-seeking, tension-reducing and, hence, ultimately retrograde libido, Freud hurls the mistletoe a second time. Like the dying and resurgent Baldr, life, as he conceives it, is an interplay of Eros and Thanatos, love and death. Moving "with vacillating rhythm … one group of instincts rushes forward so as to reach the final aim of life as swiftly as possible; but when a particular stage in the advance has been reached, the other group jerks back to a certain point to make a fresh start and so prolong the journey."[53]

---

[49] Sigmund Freud, *Moses and Monotheism*, tr. K. Jones (New York: Vintage Books, 1939).
[50] Freud, *Beyond the Pleasure Principle*, p. 34fn.
[51] Freud, *Beyond the Pleasure Principle,* pp. 34-35.
[52] Freud, *The Ego and the Id*, p. 37: "If it is true that Fechner's principle of constancy governs life, which thus consists of a continuous descent towards death, it is the claims of Eros, of the sexual instincts, which, in the form of instinctual needs, hold up the falling level and introduce fresh tensions."
[53] Freud, *Beyond the Pleasure Principle,* pp. 34-35.

Óðinn rides Sleipnir to Hel to consult the Volva

Part Two: Baldr's Jung

Baldr in Jung's Thought

We stand with our soul suspended between formidable
influences from within and from without, and somehow we
must be fair to both. This we can do only after the measure
of our individual capacities. Hence we must bethink
ourselves not so much of what we "ought" to do as of what
we *can* and *must* do.[54]

In Jung's thought, no less than in Freud's, the Baldr myth enacts itself
in the form of theories that conceive of the psyche as an ancestral soul.
Like Freud's account of archaic vestiges having come to oppress mankind
through the cultural super-ego, Jung's account of the archetypes and the
collective unconscious conceives of the psyche as having been shaped by
the experience of our forefathers through countless generations. In
contrast to Freud, however, Jung was interested less in working out the
mechanics of the process by which the ancestral soul has evolved than in
developing what might be called a participant observer's model of its
ongoing relationship with the individual psyche.

In choosing to pursue this emphasis, Jung was influenced by the same
epistemological considerations that led him to characterize psychology

---

[54] C. G. Jung, *Collected Works*, tr. R. F. C. Hull (Princeton, NJ: Princeton
University Press, 1953), vol. 7, para. 397. All subsequent references to Jung's *Collected
Works* (*CW*), vols. 1-20, will be by volume and paragraph number, designated by §.

to be a translation of the archaic speech of myth into a modern mythologem.[55] Though he, in line with Freud, spoke of the archetypes as "a deposit of phylogenetic experiences and attempts at adaptation,"[56] he was quick to add that ultimately the problem of origins is unanswerable, since everything we might think or say regarding the origin of these structures is already conditioned by them.[57] In contrast to explicative theories such as Freud's, which are doomed to fall prey to the mistletoe of their own underlying psychic assumptions, descriptive theories, such as Jung's, seek to embrace psychology's epistemological conundrum from the outset with the aim of making the underlying psychic structures in which their discourse is archetypally rooted conscious. While this approach, of course, also falls prey to the mistletoe of underlying assumptions, it is simultaneously released, as was the dying and resurgent Baldr, from identification with the projections of the various gods or psychic dominants.

Underlining passages in Jung's writings with the same pen that only moments ago had highlighted passages in the myth of Baldr and the works of Freud, we find that the quotation at the top of this section, from Jung's essay "The Relations between the Ego and the Unconscious," well conveys the Northern motif that is continued in Jung's methodological position. Lacking an Archimedean perspective, our souls are "suspended between formidable influences" emanating "from within and from without," even as Baldr was suspended in the midst of the projectile-hurling Æsir. While eschewing identification with these influences, it is salutary, according to Jung, to give them their due all the same. By remaining mindful of our "individual capacities," we may minimize servile and imitative compliance with the received imperatives of the inner and outer worlds.[58] While it would be going too far to heed the counsel of Nietzsche, who would appear to have fallen into just such a state of compliance when he bid all higher men to transform every "It was" into an "I wanted it thus,"[59] Jung speaks more modestly of doing not what we "ought" to do but "what we *can* and *must* do." In Jung's view, it is by weighing the influences and imperatives of the soul's life

---

[55] Jung, CW 9i § 302.

[56] Jung, *CW* 6 § 512.

[57] Jung, *CW* 9i § 187.

[58] Jung, *CW* 7 § 242.

[59] Friedrich Nietzsche, *Thus Spoke Zarathustra*, tr. J. Hollingdale (Harmondsworth: Penguin Books, 1961), p. 161.

against the feather of individual capacity that we liberate ourselves from the soul-obliterating hubris of sustained identification,[60] or, as this state is also called by Jung, possession.[61]

Jung's cautionary remark with respect to "what we 'ought' to do" is resonant with our previous discussion of Freud's theory of the cultural super-ego. Though Jung does not subscribe to Freud's theory, criticizing it a number of times,[62] he would certainly have agreed that it presents a vivid picture of just how formidable the ideals to which we are heir can be. Man's cultural values, pavilioned as they are upon archaic vestiges and evolutionary relics, bear in upon our souls as a crushing weight. But for Jung, as our quote suggests, this weight is a fatal burden only if we lose sight of our individual capacities and allow ourselves to become identified with these influences.

There are still other ways in which the variation of the Baldr myth that Jung provides in his theory differs from Freud's. Although he explicitly describes the collective unconscious as an underworld or land of the dead,[63] even as our Norse myth speaks of a realm called Hel, he does not imagine death as literally as Freud does with this theory of a death-instinct bent upon returning to the inert stability of the inorganic world. The archetypes, for Jung, though age-old, exert a vital and vitalizing influence upon the life of the individual today. In this regard, they bear more of a resemblance to Freud's notion of Eros than to his notion of the death-instinct, as the following text makes clear.

> ... [T]he [collective] unconscious, as the totality of all archetypes, is the deposit of all human experience right back to its remotest beginnings. Not, indeed, a dead deposit, a sort of abandoned rubbish-heap, but a living

---

[60] Cf. C. G. Jung, *Memories, Dreams, Reflections*, tr. R. & C. Winston (New York: Random House, 1965), p. 325. Here Jung returns to the theme of acting in accordance with one's individual capacities when he writes that "the feeling for the infinite ... can be attained only if we are bounded to the utmost," i.e., in a realistic sense of our personal limitations and life tasks.

[61] To be fair to Nietzsche we should recall that he also spoke of the value of "short-lived habits." Through these one may passionately live the imperatives of the unconscious without finally being possessed by them. See his *The Joyful Wisdom*, tr. T. Common (New York: Frederick Ungar Publishing, 1979), pp. 229-230.

[62] Jung, *CW* 10 § 831. In the course of critiquing Freud's notion of the super-ego, Jung comments that "the 'archaic vestiges' in the super-ego are a concession to the archetypes theory and imply a fundamental doubt as to the absolute dependence of unconscious contents on consciousness."

[63] Jung, *Memories, Dreams, Reflections*, pp. 319-320.

system of reactions and aptitudes that determine the individual's life in invisible ways …. It is not just a gigantic historical prejudice, so to speak, an *a priori* historical condition; it is also the source of the instincts, for the archetypes are simply the forms which the instincts assume. From the living fountain of instinct flows everything that is creative; hence the unconscious is not merely conditioned by history, but is the very source of the creative impulse. It is like Nature herself—prodigiously conservative, and yet transcending her own historical conditions in her acts of creation. No wonder, then, that it has always been a burning question for humanity how best to adapt to these invisible determinants.[64]

As individuals, according to Jung, we are suspended between the culturally mediated forms of our collective life and the equally collective instinctual forms which reach us from the interior depths of the unconscious via archetypal images and the so-called patterns of behaviour. While being aeons-old, these "invisible determinants" are at the same time ceaselessly contemporized through our conscious grappling with them. The proviso here, of course (as we have already heard from Jung), is that we do not allow ourselves to be assimilated to these inner and outer collective factors as to an "ought," but rather, integrate them into the fabric of our lives by cleaving to a realistic sense of our individual limitations.

The dialectical stance that Jung introduced into psychology with these reflections is succinctly summed up in two adages from William Blake: "Opposition is true Friendship" and "Without Contraries is no progression."[65] By openly recognizing and at the same time carefully distinguishing ourselves from the imperatives and spirits which approach us outwardly from what Freud called the cultural super-ego as well as inwardly from the collective unconscious, we may, according to Jung, live an individual life that is at the same time a life in accordance with the deeper trends of our psychic wholeness. As Jung expresses this in a passage in which he once again depicts the Baldr-like predicament of the individual soul,

---

[64] Jung, *CW* 8 § 339.
[65] William Blake, *Selected Poetry and Prose of Blake*, ed. N. Frye (New York: The Modern Library, 1953), pp. 123, 132.

… [S]ince the unconscious factors act as determinants no less than the factors that regulate the life of society, and are no less collective, I might just as well learn to distinguish between what *I* want and what the unconscious thrusts upon me, as to see what my office demands of me and what I myself desire. At first the only thing that is at all clear is the incompatibility of the demands coming from without and from within, with the ego standing between them, as between hammer and anvil. But over against this ego, tossed like a shuttlecock between the outer and inner demands, there stands some scarcely definable arbiter, which I would on no account label with the deceptive name "conscience," although, taken in its best sense, the word fits that arbiter very aptly indeed. …. We should do far better to realize that the tragic counterplay between inside and outside (depicted in Job and *Faust* as the wager with God) represents, at bottom, the energetics of the life process, the polar tension that is necessary for self-regulation. However different, to all intents and purposes, these opposing forces may be, their fundamental meaning and desire is the life of the individual: they always fluctuate round this centre of balance. Just because they are inseparably related through opposition, they also unite in a mediatory meaning, which, willingly or unwillingly, is born out of the individual and is therefore divined by him. He has a strong feeling of what should be and what could be. To depart from this divination means error, aberration, illness.[66]

Jung Consults the Volva

In the myth of Baldr there is a movement back and forth between the world of the living and the land of the dead. Concerned about Baldr's dreams and what they might portend for his fate and the fate of the gods in general, Óðinn visited Hel in search of answers. Later, after Baldr had been killed, Hel was visited again, this time by Hermod the Fleet, as part of an effort to bring him back to life. In the chapter "Life after Death" of his autobiography, Jung covers something of this same ground when he characterizes his entire psychological enterprise as "an attempt, ever renewed, to give an answer to the question of the interplay between the 'here' and the 'hereafter.'"[67] Like

---

[66] Jung, *CW* 7 § 311.
[67] Jung, *Memories, Dreams, Reflections*, p. 299.

Óðinn on his journey to Hel to consult with the Volva on Baldr's behalf, Jung conceived of his "confrontation with the unconscious," both on a personal and professional level, as a confrontation with the ancestral dead.[68] Riding the eight-legged horse of his active imaginations, Jung followed the introverting current of his libido into depths of an unconscious which he held to be not personal only, but collective as well. Immersed in the figures which he encountered there, even as the dying and resurgent Baldr stood in the midst of his projectile-hurling company, Jung writes,

> I frequently have a feeling that [the dead] are standing directly behind us, waiting to hear what answer we will give to them, and what answer to destiny.[69]

By sensing the presence of the dead standing directly behind him, Jung narrowed the gap between what Freud called the ego and the ego-ideal. To the extent that the "former ego-structures[,] which have left their precipitates behind in the id"[70] from time immemorial, could be imaginatively perceived and consciously reckoned with, their determining influence could be mitigated. In Jung's view, what is inherited from our ancestors need not entirely preclude what we, its heirs, would choose to inaugurate through the opportunity afforded to us by individual existence. Though the dead do pass on to us a legacy, this only manifests itself as the mounting burden of guilt which Freud described when we fail to heed it as a call to individuation.[71]

In two further passages, Jung underscores his sense of psychology as a question concerning the interplay of 'here' and 'hereafter,' an archaic myth in modern dress, a dialogue with the dead. In the first of these he conceives of psychic existence on the model of mythic accounts of the afterlife; in the second he once again, in characteristic fashion, images himself to be immersed in a consciousness-advancing tête-à-tête with interior figures.

> Psychic existence, and above all the inner images ..., supply the material for all mythic speculations about a life in the hereafter, and I imagine that life as a continuance in the world of images. Thus the psyche

---

[68] Jung, *Memories, Dreams, Reflections*, pp. 191-192; *CW* 9i § 224.
[69] Jung, *Memories, Dreams, Reflections*, p. 308.
[70] Freud, *The Ego and the Id*, p. 38.
[71] Jung, *CW* 18 § 1084-1106.

might be that existence in which the hereafter or the land of the dead is located.[72]

The dead have become ever more distinct for me as the voices of the Unanswered, Unresolved, and Unredeemed; for since the questions and demands which my destiny required me to answer did not come to me from outside, they must have come from the inner world. These conversations with the dead formed a kind of prelude to what I had to communicate to the world about the unconscious: a kind of pattern of order and interpretation of its general contents.[73]

In contrast to the materialistic dialectic through which Baldr enacts himself in Freud's explicative account of the origin and development of the ancestral soul, Jung's more descriptively conceived vision enacts that god in its deeply introverted and experiential account of the phenomena arising from the dialectic relationship between the ego and the unconscious.[74] Jung's interest, as we have already noted, was not in the causality of the cosmogonic process that produced our world and us in it. His concern, as we shall presently discuss, was with what he called the "second cosmogony."[75] With this term, Jung referred to that still unfinished act of creation that was inaugurated with the intervention of reflecting consciousness into the previously unapprehended order of things. This second cosmogony (in which the first is brought to fulfillment) continues to unfold as we, acting within the boundaries of our individual capacities, consciously distinguish ourselves from the inner and outer ordinances which continue to reach us from the dark world of the first creation.

Natural history tells us of a haphazard and casual transformation of species over hundreds of millions of years of devouring and being devoured. The biological and political history of man is an elaborate repetition of the same thing [as our discussion of Freud would attest—G. M.]. But the history of the mind offers a different picture. Here the

---

[72] Jung, *Memories, Dreams, Reflections*, pp. 319-320.
[73] Jung, *Memories, Dreams, Reflections*, pp. 191-192.
[74] Jung, *CW* 18 § 1738. "Modern psychology can no longer disguise the fact that the object of its investigation is its own essence, so that in certain respects there can be no 'principles' or valid judgements at all, but only *phenomenology*—in other words, *sheer experience.*"
[75] Jung, *Memories, Dreams, Reflections*, p. 339.

miracle of reflecting consciousness intervenes—the second cosmogony. The importance of consciousness is so great that one cannot help suspecting the element of *meaning* to be concealed somewhere within all the monstrous, apparently senseless biological turmoil, and that the road to its manifestation was ultimately found on the level of warm-blooded vertebrates possessed of a differentiated brain— found as if by chance, unintended and unforeseen, and yet somehow sensed, felt and groped for out of some dark urge.[76]

The Struggle with the Dead

But what account can be given of Jung's thought concerning the development of the ancestral soul? It is not enough to claim that Jung distanced himself from this question when his theory concerning the ongoing creative effect that the development of consciousness has upon the collective unconsciousness suggests otherwise. In this connection let us recall that Jung believed that what is really done once by an individual somewhere becomes a permanent addition to the collective soul, a new dispensation, whether for weal or woe, affecting everyone everywhere.[77]

Critics of the phylogenetic theories of Freud and Jung suggest that their theories are suspect because of a reliance on outmoded notions of genetics. Freud's account of the development of the ancestral soul, however, as we have already seen, is really not a genetic theory at all, but one that derives its logic from the Helmholzian physics of his day. In Jung's case too, despite various references to inheritance, genetics is less the mechanism by which the ancestral soul or land of the dead has come into being than is the psyche's *reaction* to genetics.[78] No critique of Jung's notion of the collective unconscious that fails to reckon with the fact that he considers the psyche to be a reality in its own right, a principle *sui generis*,[79] can lay claim to having explored this issue with any authority. Just as the psyche, for Jung, creates an asymmetrical mirror world of images by responding out of its own

---

[76] Jung, *Memories, Dreams, Reflections*, p. 339.
[77] C. G. Jung, *Letters*, vol. I: 1906-1950 & vol. II: 1951-1961, ed. G. Adler & A. Jaffé, tr. R. F. C. Hull (Princeton, NJ: Princeton University Press, 1973 & 1975), vol. I, p. 58; vol. II, p. 595.
[78] Jung, *CW* 8 § 331-332.
[79] Jung, *CW* 9, i § 117.

mysterious nature to the influences at work upon it,[80] so the ancestral soul is the asymmetrical image which the psyche has created in response to such realities as genetics, generational family history, shared complexes, human phylogeny, and the history of civilization and culture.[81] As Jung expresses this, "empirically considered ... the archetype did not ever come into existence as a phenomenon of organic life, but entered the picture with life itself."[82] All this, of course, precedes the appearance of consciousness. Predicated on the *a priori* foundation provided by the asymmetrical mirror world of the archetype, consciousness, for Jung, is a later development which enters the picture in two ways. In the first place, it is the difference between the objective outer world of nature and the equally objective interior world of psychic images that creates the dialectical tension from which consciousness is born.[83] In the second place, consciousness, that "second cosmogony," continuously contemporizes the collective unconscious by compelling it to react to the reflective awareness it brings into the order of things. Again, the proviso here is that the individual, in his role as bearer of consciousness, remain within the limits of his individual capacities. As in the science fiction film, *Back to the Future*, the ancestral soul seems to have developed in accordance with an *inverse* form of 'Lamarckian' inheritance operating on an *imaginal*, rather than genetic, level.[84] What the individual makes conscious in his life is the time machine through which the dead acquire the characteristics of their descendants even as the hero, according to Jung, braves incest to become his own father.[85] Like Baldr's dreams, Jung's vision of individuation as a soul-revolutionizing process on the brink of apocalypse also disturbs the gods. As Jung (or more likely his associate Maria Moltzer[86]) put it in an address to The Psychology Club of Zürich in which these issues are discussed,

---

[80] Jung, *CW* 4 § 665.

[81] Jung, *CW* 7 § 507. "The collective unconscious contains, or is, an historical mirror-image of the world."

[82] Jung, *CW* 11 § 222n.

[83] Jung, *Letters*, vol. I, p. 143.

[84] See my "Mourning and Metapsychology: An Archetypal View," *Spring 58: A Journal of Archetype and Culture* (Woodstock, CT: Spring Journal, 1995), pp. 51-68.

[85] Jung, *CW* 5 § 332, 335, 497, 516.

[86] Sonu Shamdasani, *Cult Fictions: C. G. Jung and the Founding of Analytical Psychology* (London: Routledge, 1998), pp. 56-75.

The separating of the personality from the collective soul seems to disturb phylogenetically certain pictures or formations in the unconscious—a process which we still understand very little, but which needs the greatest care in treatment. The struggle with the Dead is terrible, and I understand the instinct of mankind which protests against this great effort as long as it is possible to do so.[87]

Consciousness and the Child Archetype

Consciousness hedged about by psychic powers, sustained or threatened or deluded by them, is the age-old experience of mankind. This experience has projected itself into the archetype of the child, which expresses man's wholeness. The "child" is all that is abandoned and exposed and at the same time divinely powerful; the insignificant, dubious beginning, and the triumphal end. The "eternal child" in man is an indescribable experience, an incongruity, a handicap, and a divine prerogative; an imponderable that determines the ultimate worth or worthlessness of a personality.[88]

In this quotation from Jung's essay, "The Psychology of the Child Archetype," the myth of Baldr is enacted in the description that it provides of an "age-old experience of mankind." Like Baldr set up in the midst of the projectile-hurling Æsir, consciousness is described as having repeatedly experienced itself, during the course of its long history, as being "hedged about by psychic powers, sustained, threatened or deluded by them." As our text indicates, a common image of this moment in the soul's life is that of an "abandoned ... exposed and at the same time divinely powerful" child. This image, according to Jung, is figurative of consciousness inasmuch as consciousness is the "child" of the unconscious. Born of this mother and under her protection, consciousness is at the same time menaced by the prospect of being incorporated back into her again, as her womb becomes a tomb. Again, we may think of Baldr. The youngest of the Norse divinities, Baldr belongs to the mythological class of youthful consorts of the Great Mother, through his relationship to the mother-goddess, Frigg. In contrast to the very different

---

[87] Cited in Richard Noll, *The Jung Cult: Origins of a Charismatic Movement* (Princeton, N.J.: Princeton University Press, 1994), pp. 251-252.
[88] Jung, *CW* 9, i § 300.

figure of the hero, which reflects consciousness at a stage in which it is strong enough to break free from the sway of the unconscious, the son-lover figure presents consciousness in a more nascent form.[89]

The Northern light that we have just brought to bear upon Jung's account of the vicissitudes of consciousness was shone by Jung as well. In the chapter, "Symbols of the Mother and of Rebirth," of his *Symbols of Transformation*, Jung explicitly draws upon the myth of Baldr to illustrate the dynamics of the relationship between consciousness in its nascent stages of differentiation and the unconscious. Focusing upon the mistletoe, Jung reminds us that the deadliness of this plant is a function of its youth. As the myth puts it, Frigg did not require the mistletoe to swear itself harmless against Baldr because it was too young. Jung then goes on to explain that from a botanical point of view mistletoe is a parasite that lives off of a larger host tree. Completing his brief amplification he then includes several references to folklore associations linking mistletoe and fertility. The implication of all this, for Jung, is that mistletoe, as a fertile parasite living off a larger tree, tells the familiar story, even in actual nature, of the son-consort of the Great Mother. The mistletoe, for Jung, is, thus, identical with Baldr. Since both he and the plant that kills him are images of the same parasitic dependence on the mother, the scene which they enact together is representative of the fatality inherent in this archetypal pattern.

> … [T]he mistletoe which killed Baldur was "too young"; hence this clinging parasite could be interpreted as the "child of the tree." But as the tree signifies the origin in the sense of the mother, it represents the source of life, of that magical life-force whose yearly renewal was celebrated in primitive times by the homage paid to a divine son, a *puer aeternus*. The graceful Baldur is such a figure. This type is granted only a fleeting existence, because he is never anything but

---

[89] Jung's characterization of consciousness as the child of the unconscious has two main facets. In the first place, both ontogenetically and phylogenetically consciousness is regarded as being younger than the unconscious, an emanation of it as it were. In the second place, consciousness, being unable to apprehend the greater field of the unconscious, has projected its vulnerable nascent stages of development into the child archetype. As Jung (*CW* 8 § 676) writes, "… [T]he unconscious is always there beforehand as a system of inherited psychic functioning handed down from primeval times. Consciousness is a late-born descendent of the unconscious psyche. It would certainly show perversity if we tried to explain the lives of our ancestors in terms of their late descendents, and it is just as wrong, in my opinion, to regard the unconscious as just a derivative of consciousness."

an anticipation of something desired and hoped for. ... [H]e only lives on and through the mother and can strike no roots in the world, so that he finds himself in a state of permanent incest. He is, as it were, only a dream of the mother, an ideal which she soon takes back into herself .... The mistletoe, like Baldur, represents the "child of the mother," the longed-for, revivified life-force that flows from her. But, separated from its host, the mistletoe dies. ... This is the dream of the mother in matriarchal times, when there was as yet no father to stand by the side of the son.[90]

In the next paragraph, Jung extends his reflections on the Baldr myth, discussing it now in connection to the nascent stage of consciousness and its relationship to the matrix from which it has emerged, the unconscious. In answer to the question: "But why should the mistletoe kill Baldur, since it is, in a sense, his sister or brother?" he writes:

The lovely apparition of the *puer aeternus* is, alas, a form of illusion. In reality he is a parasite on the mother, a creature of her imagination, who only lives when rooted in the maternal body. In actual psychic experience the mother corresponds to the collective unconscious, and the son to consciousness, which fancies itself free but must ever again succumb to the power of sleep and deadening unconsciousness. The mistletoe, however, corresponds to the shadow brother ... whom the psychotherapist regularly meets as a personification of the personal unconscious. Just as, at evening, the shadows lengthen and finally engulf everything, so the mistletoe betokens Baldur's end. Being an equivalent of Baldur himself, it is fetched down from the tree like the "treasure hard to attain".... The shadow becomes fatal when there is too little vitality or too little consciousness in the hero for him to complete his heroic task.[91]

With these explicit references to Baldr, Jung illustrates the situation in which consciousness, according to his conception, finds itself during the nascent stages of its development. Consciousness, in his view, is the child of the pre-existing (in contrast to repressed) unconscious. Like other mythical son-consorts of the Mother Goddess, it is fatherless. By this Jung

[90] Jung, *CW* 5 § 392.
[91] Jung, *CW* 5 § 393.

seems to mean that it is lacking in effect. Without a father to stand by it, youthful consciousness is little more than a dream of the mother upon which it hangs like the parasitic mistletoe. For all its omnipotence in the realm of fantasy, little may come of it at this stage. Like the barrage of projectiles that left Baldr quite unscathed, one fantasy supplants another. Eventually, however, the situation changes. Lack of adaptation to the inner and outer worlds results in an accumulation of libido in the personal unconscious, a turn of events which then takes on a menacing character. Though protected by the mother, youthful consciousness comes more and more into conflict with the shadow. Just as the mother's boy who doesn't throw the snowball is the one that gets pelted by the other boys and then punished for being the instigator of the whole commotion, emergent consciousness eventually gets pummelled into a more differentiated awareness of its own existence by happenings which are anomalous to the mother-bound state in which subject and object are still archaically identified.

Projection and Re-Collection

These reflections bring us to the topic of projection. The reader, doubtless, has already been reminded by our frequent references to the "projectile-hurling Æsir" of this psychological phenomenon. Looking now in detail at the resemblance that exists between the Baldr myth and Jung's theory of projection, it is immediately evident that this theory is another important instance of how Jung's thought enacts the myth of Baldr. Just as our Northern myth depicts a situation in which Baldr is protected by Frigg from the objects which the Æsir throw (until the sprig of mistletoe brings this situation to an end), so Jung differentiates between what he calls "archaic identity between subject and object"[92] and projection proper. In the state of archaic identity, or as he also calls it, *participation mystique*, the objects of the world have sworn themselves harmless against the nascently conscious subject who dwells among them in a state of non-differentiation similar to that which we believe to exist in the early mother-child relationship. Though to a more developed consciousness observing such an animistic scene it would appear that it is rife with projections, Jung reserves this term for when the emergent consciousness comes into conflict with itself and/

---

[92] Jung, *CW* 6 § 783.

Ancestral bowmen convey the notion of archetypal projection

or its situation.[93] Only then is it proper to pluck the mistletoe and speak of projection.

> Projection results from the archaic *identity* of subject and object, but is properly so called only when the need to dissolve the identity with the object has already arisen. This need arises when the identity becomes a disturbing factor, i.e., when the absence of the projected content is a hindrance to adaptation and its withdrawal into the subject has become desirable. From this moment the previous partial identity acquires the character of projection. The term projection therefore signifies a state of identity that has become noticeable, an object of criticism, whether it be the self-criticism of the subject or objective criticism of another.[94]

The reference in the last sentence of this quotation about criticism having two possible objects, an inner one which gives rise to self-criticism and an outer one which gives rise to what Jung calls "objective criticism of another," brings us back to our earlier discussion of the place of consciousness between inner and outer forces from which it must differentiate itself. Like Baldr in the midst of the objects hurled at him by the Æsir, ego-consciousness, for Jung, as a "relatively constant personification of the unconscious,"[95] assimilates and is assimilated to the inner and outer objects which the unconscious animates. To a nascent consciousness the picture here is one of ceaseless incest or archaic identity. For a more developed consciousness, one that has already by means of critical judgements differentiated itself from the unconscious, the picture is that of a one-sided development. Like the king in alchemy who becomes so swollen with dropsy that he eventually is dissolved on that account,[96] the ego may assimilate to itself more than it can finally contain. At this point the difference between assimilation and integration becomes clear, as does the associated difference between archaic identity and projection. Far from being the integral centre of the world (as the scene of Baldr set up as the happy target of the gods might suggest), the ego has merely been assimilating contents one-sidedly, which is to say, on behalf of a

---

[93] In analysis, the shift from *participation mystique* to critical awareness of projection is often accompanied by dreams in which a weapon-bearing army appears, or war has broken out.

[94] Jung, *CW* 6 § 783.

[95] Jung, *CW* 14 § 129.

[96] Jung, *CW* 14 § 358-361.

dominant which it has failed to criticize and is therefore unconsciously identical with. It is only when such an ego is burst asunder and must actually face its root assumptions and change its foundations that it is proper to speak of a projection's having been grappled with and integrated. Expressed more anciently, in the 'psychoanalytic terms' of our Northern myth, Baldr's dreams of his own demise frighten the gods because they presage the apocalyptic Ragnarök, to which they too are doomed.[97]

Heroic Incest

For Jung, it is by identifying briefly with the archetype of the hero that consciousness begins to differentiate itself out from that more primordial state of archaic identity which is reflected in mythology by such son-consort figures as Baldr. Although identification with the hero brings about an identification with a dominant of the collective unconscious that will at some time need to be sacrificed, it may initially well serve the emergence of ego-consciousness as it navigates a whole series of encounters with the unconscious. As Jung puts it (and here let us keep in mind the image of Baldr receiving the projectiles which the Æsir mirthfully hurl at him): "The teleological significance of the hero as a symbolic figure who attracts libido to himself in the form of wonder and adoration ... lead[s] it over the symbolic bridge of myth to higher uses ...."[98]

Another passage from the same work may be read alongside this one (once again with the scene from our Northern myth in mind) to give a more complete picture of ego's heroic capacity to critique, sacrifice, and transform its incestuous dependency upon the unconscious.

> The canalization of regressive libido into the god justifies the mythological statement that it is the god or the hero who commits incest. On the primitive level no further symbolization is required. This only becomes necessary when the mythological statement begins to bring the god into discredit, which obviously only happens at a higher level of morality.[99]

---

[97] At a similar juncture, Jesus took pains to reassure the old gods. In the same breath as he inaugurated, through the moral critique of his exemplary life, a new dispensation (thereby bringing to an end the former state of archaic identity), he declared that he had not come to destroy the law or the prophets but to fulfill them. Cf. Matthew 5:17.

[98] Jung, *CW* 5 § 477. Sense slightly altered.

[99] Jung, *CW* 5 § 390.

Read as a variant of the myth of Baldr, the phrase "canalization of regressive libido into the god" is transparent to the mythical image of Baldr as the recipient of the objects which have been obliged by Frigg not to harm him. As a mythic representation of the way things happen, this image prefigures, underpins, and exemplifies Jung's later concept of psychological incest, or as he also refers to this, *participation mystique*, the archaic identity of subject and object.

The last line of the above quotation is reminiscent of the images of our Northern myth having to do with Baldr's ultimate vulnerability and fatal wounding. Indeed, the scene in which the blind Hod, at Loki's biding, brings death to Baldr by hurling the fatal mistletoe at him is enacted in Jung's concept of a god being brought into discredit at a higher level of morality.

The development of consciousness, for Jung, is a function of continuous moral conflict. Poised between the inner and outer worlds, pelted with the demands of both, the ego, as we discussed above, must do justice to both and yet lose itself to neither. In one situation it must sacrifice the imperatives of the outer world to values that approach it from within. In another situation is must actualize itself through precisely the opposite choice. Guiding the ego in its choices is the dim presentiment of wholeness which it experiments at embodying in this way. Resistances, of course, arise and complicate this picture. The ego gets overpowered by inner figures; in its son-lover and heroic phases by the mother, at other stages by other figures. Instead of coming into possession of the consciousness that can be drawn from its brief archetypal identifications (as these are subjected to criticism and sacrificed), it becomes possessed by a single one. But the triumph it appears to have won soon shows itself to be unsustainable. Gained at the cost of dissociation from the other psychic dominants, it will eventually dwindle, like the rootless mistletoe, for all life is ultimately rooted in the manifold depths of the unconscious.

Voluntary Sacrifice

While continuing to bear in mind the scene of our myth in which the Æsir resist relinquishing the dead Baldr, let us now examine a passage from Jung's writings in which he deals with the theme of sacrifice:

> ... [A]s soon as we feel ourselves slipping, we begin to combat this tendency and erect barriers against the dark,

rising flood of the unconscious and its enticements to regression, which all too easily takes on the deceptive guise of sacrosanct ideals, principles, beliefs, etc. If we wish to stay on the heights we have reached, we must struggle all the time to consolidate our consciousness and its attitude. But we soon discover that this praiseworthy and apparently unavoidable battle with the years leads to stagnation and desiccation of soul. ... [E]ach of us has a tendency to become an immovable pillar of the past. Nevertheless, the daemon throws us down, makes us traitors to our ideals and cherished convictions—traitors to the selves we thought we were. That is an unmitigated catastrophe, because it is an *unwilling* sacrifice. Things go very differently when the sacrifice is a voluntary one. Then it is no longer an overthrow, ... the destruction of all that we held sacred, but transformation and conservation.[100]

In this passage, Jung uses concepts such as sacrifice, regression, and the unconscious to depict something of the same psychic scenario that the mythic account of Baldr's death depicts in terms of personified figures. Like the situation imaged in our Northern myth, the message is a simple one: consciousness must recognize that all the things that it becomes identified with sooner or later become redundant and pass away. As Jung expresses this in another place, this time with reference to an image resembling the mistletoe of our myth, "Like a projectile flying to its goal, life ends in death. Even its ascent and its zenith are only steps and means to this goal."[101] Just as Loki brings the mistletoe to bear upon a youthful god who has become attached to the objects of the world that have been hurled at him by the joyful Æsir, so Jung suggests that consciousness will fall prey to catastrophic compensations if it fails to make timely enough sacrifices of its archaic identity with the objects. "In the act of sacrifice," writes Jung, "... consciousness gives up its power and possessions in the interests of the unconscious. This makes possible a union of opposites resulting in a release of energy."[102]

Jung's account of the necessity of sacrifice in the development of consciousness maps the same psychological territory as Freud's account of the gap between the ego and the ego ideal, even as Baldr enacts himself

---

[100] Jung, *CW* 5 § 553.
[101] Jung, *CW* 8 § 803.
[102] Jung, *CW* 5 § 671.

in the thought of both these theorists. And yet, their visions are so different. Freud, conceiving of the psyche in an extroverted fashion, located the genesis of the psyche in the subtle continuation of earlier states of things which it is unable to detach itself from due to the negentropic physics to which it is heir. Jung, by contrast, conceiving of the psyche in an introverted fashion and confining himself to the experiences of developing consciousness, finds in renunciation and sacrifice the basis of the ego's optimal relationship with the unconscious. In Jung's view, the so-called ego-ideals, which compel the ego to achieve in some form what has been lost but not relinquished, must be carefully differentiated from the ego and subjected to criticism. Or said another way, the ego must bring criticism to bear upon itself in order to differentiate itself from the dominant of the unconscious with which it is identified. The picture here is not, as in Freud, of a long process of psychic phylogeny culminating in a civilization oppressed with discontents, but of a series of individual encounters with collective representations which can actually have a redemptive effect upon the dominants of the ancestral soul.

As in the association experiment, the individual may recognize the alterity of his identifications and interior encounters in the form of disturbances to his attention or to his ability to direct his awareness.[103] Life, itself, in Jung's view, may be compared to an association experiment, inasmuch as it pelts us with events which trouble us even as the experiment pelts us with words that make us react in peculiarly inhibited ways.[104] Again and again, we find ourselves in that typical situation, "hedged about by psychic powers, sustained or threatened or deluded by them." As Jung, relating this situation to the process of individuation puts it, "Nobody who finds himself on the road to wholeness can escape that characteristic suspension which is the meaning of crucifixion. For he will infallibly run into things that thwart and 'cross' him: first, the thing he has no wish to be (the shadow); second, the thing he is not (the 'other,' the individual reality of a 'You'); and third, his psychic non-ego (the collective unconscious)."[105] This list is not exhaustive. One could expand the encounter with the collective unconscious into a number of typical figures, such as the anima/animus and mana-

---

[103] Jung, *CW* 2 § 939-998.
[104] Jung, *CW* 2 § 895.
[105] Jung, *CW* 16 § 470.

personality.[106] Also noteworthy in this connection are Jung's views on literal ancestor possession.[107]

Inflation, Differentiation, and Actualization

We shall not undertake to discuss here the dynamics involved in the encounters between the ego and the various figures which approach it inwardly from the unconscious and outwardly through the workings of society and fate. It is enough to say that Jung describes a process in which the ego no sooner achieves differentiation from one figure than it succumbs to inflation through identification with a subsequent one.[108] Once it has stripped the anima of her fascinating power and obtained what would at first appear to be a greater handle on the unconscious, the ego becomes inflated with her mana and, aggrandized thereby, at risk of losing all that it has gained.[109] If, however, it can once again bring criticism to bear upon its inflated state,[110] and

---

[106] Scholars of Northern myth and religion have been struck by the great difference between Snorri Sturluson's account of the Baldr myth and the account of Saxo Grammaticus. Unable to unify the different stories, they have tended to explain the difference in terms of different sources. Though this may be so, there is, nevertheless, a commonality between the two portraits of this god when viewed from the perspective of the concepts in Jung's thought in which Baldr enacts himself. In Saxo's version of the myth, Baldr is a warrior-god who battles a mortal who is his foe with respect to the pursuit of a particular woman. After many battles, Baldr is finally killed by this enemy. In Jung's thought Saxo's Baldr enacts himself in the theory of the ego's inflationary encounter with the anima (and animus). Like the Æsir who pelt Baldr in Snorri's version of the myth, the anima, for Jung, not only personifies the collective unconscious (*CW* 7 § 521), but may be regarded as a representation the projection-making factor itself (*CW* 9i § 20). It is by telling in different ways a story that Jung once again tells differently in his theory of projection and the anima that there can be said to be a rough equivalence between Snorri's tale of Baldr pelted by the gods and Saxo's tale of Baldr enamoured of a woman and at war for her with another man. That Baldr is a god and his foe a mortal maps something of the same territory as does Jung's discussion of the mana-personality which appears alongside the anima. Just as the mortal foe of Baldr must grapple with this powerful God, so the ego, in its encounter with the anima (or animus), must grapple simultaneously with the mana-personality to which it may subsequently fall into identification (*CW* 7 § 374-406).

[107] C. G. Jung, *Analytical Psychology: Notes of the Seminar Given in 1925*, ed. W. McGuire (Princeton, N.J.: Princeton University Press, 1989), pp. 37, 82, 130. See also Jung, *CW* 9i: 224.

[108] Jung, *CW* 7 § 376-382.

[109] Jung, *CW* 7 § 376-382.

[110] Jung, *Letters*, vol. I, p. 227: "... [F]ree will only exists within the limits of consciousness. Beyond those limits, there is mere compulsion." Compulsion, here, means, possession by inner and outer forces, archetypal powers, historical and cultural processes, the ancestors. Only as we distinguish ourselves from these determinants is the unconscious affected by our increased consciousness.

then act within the boundaries of its individual human reality, more of the collective unconscious will be integrated and the evolution of consciousness furthered thereby.[111] It is these developments, born of the effect of consciousness upon the collective unconscious that Jung had in mind when, expressing these ideas in a religious metaphor, he wrote that "whoever knows God has an effect upon him"[112] and that "the encounter with the creature changes the creator."[113]

In our Northern myth, Baldr is at one and the same time the focal point at which the projectiles of the gods are directed, a disturbed dreamer, a reluctant sacrifice, the end of the gods, and the presiding spirit of the new creation in which we humans dwell. This constellation of images is particularly resonant with a passage from Jung's writings which we shall now quote in order to draw together and summarize our previous discussion of his thought. The passage is taken from his lecture, "Transformation Symbolism of the Mass." Immediately preceding it is the lucid discussion of the meaning of sacrifice, from which we quoted above. Concluding this earlier discussion, Jung writes that through "sacrifice we gain ourselves—our 'self'—for we have only what we give. But what does the self gain? We see it entering into manifestation, freeing itself from unconscious projection, and, as it grips us, entering into our lives and so passing from unconsciousness into consciousness, from potentiality into actuality. What it is in the diffuse unconscious state we do not know; we only know that in becoming ourselves it has become man."[114] Here is the passage, italicized to bring out the phrases in which the Baldr myth enacts itself most vividly:

> *The process of becoming human is represented in dreams and inner images as the putting together of many scattered units, and sometimes as the gradual emergence and clarification of something that was always there.*

---

[111] In the contrary case, where the ancestral mana-personality usurps the ego, the reverse results. Unwilling or unable to sacrifice its identification with the god which it has been compelled to ape, the ego-personality becomes instead its unwilling sacrificial victim. As Jung expresses it, "An inflated consciousness is always egocentric and conscious of nothing but its own existence. It is incapable of learning from the past, incapable of understanding contemporary events, and incapable of drawing right conclusions about the future. It is hypnotized by itself and therefore cannot be argued with. It inevitably dooms itself to calamities that must strike it dead" (*CW* 12 § 563).

[112] Jung, *CW* 11 § 617.

[113] Jung, *CW* 11 § 686.

[114] Jung, *CW* 11 § 398.

> ... [T]he integration or humanization of the self is
> initiated from the conscious side by our making ourselves aware
> of our selfish aims; we examine our motives and try
> to form as complete and objective a picture as possible.... *It
> is an act of self-recollection, a gathering together of what is
> scattered, of all the things in us that have never been properly
> related, and a coming to terms with oneself with a view to
> achieving full consciousness.* (Unconscious self-sacrifice is
> merely an accident, not a moral act.) *Self-recollection, however,
> is about the hardest and most repellent thing there is for man,
> who is predominantly unconscious. Human nature has an
> invincible dread of becoming more conscious of itself* [i.e., of
> dying into a fuller and more conscious life through the
> sacrifice of its identifications—G. M.]. *What nevertheless
> drives us to it is the self, which demands sacrifice by sacrificing
> tself to us. Conscious realization or the bringing together of
> scattered parts is in one sense an act of the ego's will, but in
> another sense it is a spontaneous manifestation of the self,* which
> was always there. *Individuation appears, on the one hand, as
> the synthesis of a new unity which previously consisted of scattered
> particles, and on the other hand, as the revelation of something
> which existed before the ego* and is in fact its father or creator
> and also its totality.[115]

Menacing the entire individuation process for Jung is the danger of
the ego's being assimilated to the self rather than being brought to
conscious realization. Recounting an experience of his own in which he
was brought perilously close to such a state of being, Jung told the
audience of a seminar given in 1925 of an experience he had had, while
engaged in the self-analytic practice of active imagination, of what he
calls self-deification. Immersed in his mythological studies, Jung was
pelted from without by the subject matter he was reading at that time
and from within by the affects that this material constellated within
him.[116] Like Baldr, he became the focal point at which these archetypal
projections were being directed, his ego becoming the place of their re-
collection. Having brought a measure of criticism to bear upon a
seductive feminine figure he called Salome, he then put his trust in the

---

[115] Jung, *CW* 11 § 399-400.
[116] Jung, *Analytical Psychology*, p. 92: As Jung explained to the audience of his 1925
seminar, "I had read much mythology before this fantasy came to me, and all of this
reading entered into the condensation of these figures."

evidently more trustworthy figure of Elijah who appeared in his vision
with her. And "then a most disagreeable thing happened—

> ... [Salome] began to worship me. I said, "Why do you
> worship me?" She replied, "You are Christ." In spite of my
> objections she maintained this. I said, "This is madness,"
> and became filled with sceptical resistance. Then I saw the
> snake approaching me. She came close and began to encircle
> me and press me in her coils. ... I realized as I struggled,
> that I had assumed the attitude of the Crucifixion. In the
> agony and the struggle, I sweated so profusely that the water
> flowed down on all sides of me. Then [blind] Salome rose,
> and she could see. While the snake was pressing me, I felt
> that my face had taken on the face of an animal of prey, a
> lion or a tiger.[117]

On the positive side, according to Jung, an experience of self-deification
such as this one can instill a sense of immortal value in the individual
who experiences it.[118] It was for this reason that being likened to a hero
or a deity was a basic feature of mystery initiations. On the negative side,
however, the ego may be torn asunder in madness if it is not able finally
to sacrifice such an identification. Jung's subsequent writings, particularly
the section of his *Two Essays in Analytical Psychology* dealing with the
mana-personality, clearly indicate that he worked his experience of self-
deification through to a human conclusion.[119] Recognizing with Jung
that the mana with which one has been ecstatically cathected is not one's
personal possession, but an archetypal energy, one is returned to oneself
transformed. Just as Baldr, freighted with the projectiles of the gods, was
finally given over to the realm of the dead, so the afflux of archetypal
libido is given back to the unconscious. The upshot of this, according
to Jung, is that the ego, having by means of a dialectical attitude
individuated itself out from numerous inner and outer principalities and
powers, gives way as the central psychic value to a new psychic centre
about which it revolves as does the earth about the sun.[120] This centre,
which Jung calls the self, is conceived as being equidistant between
conscious and unconscious and characterized as "a kind of compensation

---

[117] Jung, *Analytical Psychology*, p. 96.
[118] Jung, *Analytical Psychology*, p. 97.
[119] Jung, *CW* 7 § 374-406.
[120] Jung, *CW* 7 § 405.

of the conflict between inside and outside."[121] And here again we find Jung's vision of the way things happen in the psyche prefigured in the vision of our Northern myth. For it is precisely in   l this freeing of the self through the arduous process of taking back projections and then sacrificing the power which has been falsely appropriated thereby that the resurgent Baldr returns after the twilight of the gods to preside over a renewed humanity on the conceptual level of Jung's thought.

The Moment of the Ancestor between Fate and Destiny

> In the end it boils down to this: is one prepared to break with tradition, to be "unhistorical" in order to make history, or not? No one can make history who is not willing to risk everything for it, to carry the experiment with his own life through to the bitter end, and to declare that his life is not a continuation of the past, but a new beginning. Mere continuation can be left to the animals, but inauguration is the prerogative of man, the one thing he can boast of that lifts him above the beasts.[122]

Self-realization, according to Jung, is both the recognition of one's rootedness in the ancestral soul and an ahistorical break with tradition. In the case of a personality which has lagged behind the level of differentiation already achieved by the collective, the encounter with inner and outer forces will be largely compensatory and collective institutions such as the Church will mediate these compensations to the individual in the form of moral precepts or liturgical symbols. Other personalities, however, having, through the integration of projections, moved beyond the state of archaic identity in which the collective soul slumbers in their day, may exert, through their ahistorical acts of individuation-actualizing choice, a compensatory influence upon the collective unconscious. Like Baldr, their dreams will disturb the gods. And, again, like that dying and resurgent Northern deity, their integration of archetypal projections will bring about the Ragnarök or end of the gods.

It was to the needs of these latter individuals that Jung's psychology was particularly addressed. As Jung writes, "Among neurotics, there are not a few who do not require any reminders of their social duties and

---

[121] Jung, *CW* 7 § 404.
[122] Jung, *CW* 10 § 268.

The Ragnarök—the final conflagration, the end of the gods

obligations, but are born and destined rather to be bearers of new cultural ideals ....."[123] The burden of guilt which Freud saw as increasing alongside the advance of civilization Jung saw as a call to individuation. Those who do not lag behind the ethical level of their society, and yet suffer from a neurosis, may be suffering a problem that is not exclusive to them personally. At first, of course, they may not have the least awareness of this. Like Thor in Útgarða-Loki's castle, they may struggle to lift the cat off the palace floor, not realizing that it is not a cat at all but the dread Midgard Serpent, which encircles the world. The marital conflict, the apparently

---

[123] Jung, *CW* 4 § 658.

personal grievance against parents, the feelings of abandonment, of neglect, may, in the same way, be collective problems, personal encounters in which the individual confronts the myth we are all in.

When such is the case, one may dream dreams like Baldr's—ancestor dreams.[124] Or, said another way, having come of age in this recognition, one may relate to one's dreams in a different way—finding in them not only wise, compensatory commentaries on current dilemmas, but a legacy of questions and quandaries which our forebears have passed down to us. In this connection we may recall that it was the same Jung who was consulted by "the dead [who] came back from Jerusalem, where they found not what they sought"[125] that wrote: "we find among our patients individuals called to advance civilization."[126]

The writings of our analytic forebears, Freud and Jung, may be read in the same manner—runically, as if they, too, were ancestral dreams. By imagining the ways in which the divinities of the ancient North have enacted themselves in their thought, we grapple, perhaps better than they did, with the issues that drove them apart. Such, at any rate, has been the aim of the present study. By reflecting the conceptualizations over which the ways of Freud and Jung divided in the mythical images of Thor's hammer, Barnstock's progeny, and Baldr's death, we have endeavoured to return the mana with which these giants conflictually cathected each other to the Valhalla of that archetype which psychology, as the "*living and lived myth*" of our time, continues by other means.

---

[124] For an example of such a dream and further discussion of what I have called "the moment of the ancestor," see my "Of Brothels, Gambling-Hells, and the Salons of the Elegant: Collectivity, Individuality, and the Dream," *Quadrant: Journal of the C. G. Jung Foundation for Analytical Psychology*, XXXIV:1 Winter 2004, pp. 38-40.

[125] Jung, *Memories, Dreams, Reflections*, p. 378.

[126] Jung, *CW* 4 § 667.

Index